HIGHER GROUND

Ascending Ephesians, verse by verse

HIGHER GROUND

Ascending Ephesians, verse by verse

Clark Logan

RITCHIE

John Ritchie Publishing

40 Beansburn, Kilmarnock, Scotland

ISBN-13: 978 1 912522 91 0

Copyright © 2020 by John Ritchie Ltd.
40 Beansburn, Kilmarnock, Scotland

www.ritchiechristianmedia.co.uk

Typeset by John Ritchie Ltd., Kilmarnock
Printed by Bell & Bain Ltd., Glasgow

In memory of Jim and Irene Legge

'SETLHOA'
In Botswana, the thatched roof of a traditional home is capped
with a metal cone known as a *setlhoa*. It means a high point or peak.
When preaching, we also use the term freely to speak of God's blessings.
There are many such peaks in the letter to the Ephesians.

Contents

Preface

A South African friend was telling me of his visit to Northern Ireland. 'They took me to see your famous Mountains of Mourne ...' He paused and smiled. The message was clear. Accustomed as he was to the Drakensberg mountain range in South Africa, our beloved Mountains of Mourne must have seemed like molehills. Mafadi, the highest peak in South Africa, is four times higher than Slieve Donard.

In his letter to the Ephesians, the apostle Paul takes us much higher, figuratively speaking, than the Mournes or even the Drakensbergs. We find ourselves ascending the majestic Himalayas of spiritual truth. The apostle's thoughts and language soar far above the earth to encompass 'the heavenlies'. He presents to us a panoramic view of God's purposes for time and eternity. We learn of His purposes for Christ, the Church, the Christian, and the whole of Creation. All of these purposes are according to His sovereign will, and for His glory and pleasure.

It is sometimes claimed that those who are heavenly-minded are of no earthly use. Paul would disagree. In Ephesians, he applies his lofty teaching to our lowly walk here upon earth. He also shows that Christians are in a relentless spiritual battle, and the heavenly truth they learn must be worked out here and now. By this measure, it is only those who are heavenly-minded who will be of any earthly use. Paul desires that we will rise higher, as well as walk straighter, shine brighter, and stand firmer.

The format of this book on Ephesians is to consider every verse consecutively. The aim is to uncover the essential truth of Paul's letter and to present its teaching in a clear, concise, and practical way.

There are several challenges presented in this approach. Firstly, every verse in the English Bible does not have equal weight in terms of doctrine or teaching. Some may be short linking verses. Nevertheless, the hope is that you will discover *every verse has value* to spiritually nourish and sustain you throughout the day. Secondly, moving verse by verse, we could risk 'not seeing the wood for the trees'. We must be careful to keep the main themes and thought flow in mind; preview sections will help to maintain the overall picture and context.

I wish to thank Mr John Fleck of Buckna and Mr Alasdair Baijal of Cape Town who gave generously of their time and effort in reading through the complete manuscript and making valuable suggestions. John was also kind enough to write the Foreword. Also, my thanks must go to the friends at 'Ritchie's' for their unfailing assistance in easing the pathway to publication.

The volume you now hold in your hand comes with the prayer that you will be edified, encouraged, and challenged. Make sure you read it with your open Bible beside you. Begin the journey today, and keep climbing higher. It will be worth the effort to reach the summit – enjoy the view!

Clark Logan
Tlokweng
Botswana
January 2020

Foreword

It has often been remarked that some of the Bible's sixty-six books have received only scant attention from commentators, and for the general reader to receive ready help upon these parts of scripture proves rather difficult. This observation cannot be made regarding Paul's letter to the Ephesians. This letter has moved many a writer to lift his pen or go to his keyboard, and today there exists a large variety of works on Ephesians, ranging from the voluminous tomes of the puritans to the modest but helpful short commentaries of more recent times. There is a place for all of these, but many works are pretty inaccessible to the average Christian reader, and the vast majority of us must confess that we fall into this category!

This is exactly why this publication, aptly titled *Higher Ground*, will be a very appropriate addition to your bookshelf or coffee table. Dr Clark Logan has 'the pen of a ready writer', giving to us over the years a number of works that have proved valuable, timely, and always characterised by something not easily achieved – a smooth and stimulating readability. Our attention is held by the writer's down-to-earth realism, as he punctuates his work with vivid applications, anecdotes, and lessons drawn from the everyday situations of life. Many years of moving amongst people in the service of the Lord, not least in his beloved African mission field, has given him the required insight, wisdom and sensitivity to render the further service which this volume represents. This is far removed from the sometimes cold and clinical treatments of Bible books, which never seem to touch the soul or move us towards greater likeness to our Lord Jesus Christ.

Paul's letter to the Ephesians stands in first place amongst his four prison epistles, at least in Biblical order. The Lord's letter to the Ephesians stands in first place amongst the seven to the churches of Asia in

Revelation. It may be just a flight of personal fancy, but I think many will allow me to draw from this a sense that Ephesians commands a place of primacy in our thoughts as Christians. It is inspired scripture of course, but the human writer chosen by God to take the pen has given to the world this precious document as the product of his matured understanding of the ways of God. Paul's years of acquaintance with his Lord and the opportunity afforded by the quietness of the prison have resulted in this sublime epistle. He unfolds the greatness of God's eternal purpose in Christ, and the exalted position the Church has in its relationship to Christ. He will one day be Head over all things, but even now He is already Head over the Church. The exceeding riches of God's grace has elevated us into such a favoured position, and He will display this grace to a wondering universe. In the meantime, such lofty doctrines must have an effect upon our daily walk as believers.

These two things, doctrine and practice, have been kept in very useful balance in this volume. The verse-by-verse approach is reader friendly and keeps things manageable and memorable as we move through the epistle. It has been my pleasure to read through the manuscript, and I am confident that every other reader will be blessed of God as I have been. In its publication, the words of Ephesians 3.21 are fitting: "Unto Him be glory in the church by Christ Jesus, throughout all ages, world without end. Amen."

John Fleck
Buckna
Northern Ireland
January 2020

Introduction

In the first century, Ephesus was a large and influential city. On the commercial side, its inland harbour was the main point of entrance for all sea traffic to the Roman province of Asia Minor, now part of Turkey. It was thus the gateway to the east. On the cultural side, it was home to the magnificent Temple of Diana, the fertility goddess; this edifice was one of the wonders of the ancient world. The amphitheatre in the city could hold 25,000 people. Ephesus was therefore a prosperous but idolatrous place where the people were also known to practise magic arts. Apart from the records of general history and the letter we are now studying, there are several Bible references that provide background information on the work of God that developed there.

Through the grace of God and by the power of the gospel, many lives were transformed in Ephesus. Dr Luke, in Acts 18-19, graphically portrays the early days of gospel advance in the city: there was blessing but also opposition, particularly from the business community. The city merchants were losing out on their sales of silver shrines to Diana as new believers publicly renounced their involvement with the occult and idolatry. Many of them suffered because of their faith in Christ. In Acts 20, we have a record of the last meeting Paul had with the elders of the Ephesian church. His poignant words mingled with tears summed up his ministry among them and his hopes for them. He also warned them of challenges to come. Paul's younger co-worker, Timothy, would later serve the believers in the city; Paul also wrote a personal letter to him to encourage him in the challenges he faced there (1 Tim 1.3).

Paul was under house arrest in Rome (AD 61-63) when he wrote his letter to the Ephesian Christians. He spoke of divine purposes, blessings, and love. He extolled the greatness of God's love (Eph 2.4), the costliness of Christ's love (Eph 5.2), and the testimony of the believers' love (Eph

1.15). A generation later, the local church at Ephesus received through the apostle John another divine communication in letter form (Rev 2.1-11). It also had to do with love, but the years had brought changes, and the spiritual condition of the believers needed reviving.

Paul wrote this letter out of a heart burdened with concern for the welfare of those believers he cared for so dearly. It divides simply in this way:

Chs. 1-3 RICHES IN CHRIST   Chs. 4-6 RESPONSIBILITIES IN CHRIST

1 Blessedness in Christ   4 Walk straighter
2 Nearness in Christ   5 Shine brighter
3 Richness in Christ   6 Stand firmer

(God's purposes concerning our wealth, our walk, our witness, and our warfare.)

Chapter 1

Blessedness in Christ

After greeting the Christians at Ephesus,
Paul praises God for all of the believers' blessings in Christ.
He then prays that the Ephesian believers might know
and understand these blessings.

1.1 - A Man on a Mission

Paul, an apostle of Jesus Christ by the will of God, to the saints which are at Ephesus, and to the faithful in Christ Jesus:

Paul identified himself as the writer. His apostleship was not something he had achieved but a commission he had been given by the risen Lord. In common with the other apostles, he had seen the Lord, but unlike the rest, he had a special personal encounter with Him on the Damascus Road (Acts 9.1-9); this occurred several years after Christ's resurrection and ascension.

Right at the beginning of this letter, God's purposes are brought to the fore, not just for His people in general, but for each believer in particular. God's will for Paul's life had been made clear to him by the Lord: to be "a chosen vessel unto me, to bear my name before the Gentiles, and kings, and the children of Israel: For I will shew him how great things he must suffer for my name's sake" (Acts 9.15-16). Paul never looked back; he devoted the rest of his life to fulfilling his commission.

The intended recipients of his letter were the Christians in Ephesus. They were described in two ways – as the saints, and as the faithful. To be a saint refers to one's position as having been set apart for God. This takes place at the moment of conversion; indeed, God calls every believer a saint. Saints do not suddenly become sinlessly perfect at conversion, but they take up the challenge to begin living out what God has made them.

Their position as being those separated unto God was reflected in their spiritual condition. These two aspects are seen in the division of the letter (Chs. 1-3 positional; Chs. 4-6 practical). Faith in Christ is demonstrated by faithfulness to Christ. This implies a lifelong commitment to honour the Lord by being obedient to His Word and being diligent in His work. No doubt Paul was encouraged to be able to describe the Ephesian believers in this way.

The sphere of their spiritual position and activity was "in Christ Jesus". They were vitally linked to Him who had become their Saviour and Lord. The change of word order may be significant. The first, Jesus

Christ, focuses on the One who lived down here upon earth, who is now exalted up there in heaven. The second, Christ Jesus, is a reminder that the Christ of heaven humbled Himself to become Jesus who lived and served among men. This was the One who was their Lord and Master.

In Christ, we are saints, but are we faithful?

1.2 - Grace and Peace

Grace be to you, and peace, from God our Father, and from the Lord Jesus Christ.

Readers of the New Testament letters of Paul will be familiar with this short greeting. Paul combines both Greek and Jewish elements although he replaces the usual Greek word of introduction, 'Rejoice!', with the much fuller word, 'Grace'. Shalom, meaning peace, remains the traditional Hebrew greeting to this day.

'Grace' would have to be one of Paul's favourite words; all his letters begin and end with it. In the same way his whole Christian life, from the time of his conversion to his impending death, was bracketed by grace. Speaking of his unlikely conversion, and recalling his persecution of the early Church, he described himself as having been "a blasphemer, and a persecutor, and injurious: but I obtained mercy ... and the grace of our Lord was exceeding abundant with faith and love which is in Christ Jesus" (1 Tim 1.13-14). As to his ministry, he could confess that "by the grace of God I am what I am: and his grace which was bestowed upon me was not in vain; but I laboured more abundantly than they all: yet not I, but the grace of God which was with me" (1 Cor 15.10). It is through grace that God blesses the undeserving.

It has been well remarked that grace must always come before peace. Without God's grace, there can never be peace in a sinner's heart. There is little peace in the world but the Christian's peace is within and does not depend upon external circumstances. It is peace with

God, and the enjoyment of knowing the forgiveness of every sin, daily fellowship with the Lord, and the sure and certain hope of a home in heaven. It is the peace of knowing that the Lord is in control of every circumstance; when trials come, one can still feel safe in the eye of the storm. On his way to Rome and under armed guard, Paul was once caught up in a real and terrible storm at sea, and he was the only one at peace. He knew his God and could offer words of comfort: "be of good cheer: for I believe God, that it shall be even as it was told me" (Acts 27.25). All the passengers, 276 souls, made it safely ashore.

The familiar linking of God the Father with the Lord Jesus Christ reminds us that Jesus Christ is the Son of God. The verse affirms unity and equality in the Godhead.

Peace in the storms of life can be ours when the Lord is by our side.

1.3 - Blessed in Christ

Blessed be the God and Father of our Lord Jesus Christ, who hath blessed us with all spiritual blessings in heavenly places in Christ:

Paul begins by 'blessing' God. The specific word used here appears eight times in the New Testament where it always refers to praise Godward, in recognition of who He is. The first long paragraph (vv. 3-14) is one continuous sentence, being a fervent outpouring of praise to God. It is always good and right to bless God for who He is, even before blessing Him for what He has done. This signifies spiritual maturity, when the Giver is appreciated just as much as His gifts.

God is described as the Father of our Lord Jesus Christ, further emphasising the intimate and eternal relationship of Father and Son in the Godhead. They are equal in power and glory, but through the coming into the world of Jesus Christ, His deity was robed with humanity, and God was manifested in flesh. The Father sent the Son to be the Saviour of the world (1 Jn 4.14), and in perfect obedience Christ came and fulfilled His Father's will (Jn 6.38).

God has blessed His children abundantly and in Christ He has provided them with all that they need. The sphere of the believer's spiritual blessings is "in the heavenlies" (Eph 1.3 JND). This phrase is unique to Ephesians and occurs another four times in the letter (Eph 1.20; 2.6; 3.10; 6.12). It reaches beyond earth altogether and reminds us of a spirit world above. It cannot be confined to a particular place or even heaven, the dwelling place of God, because it also refers to the sphere of the believers' enemies and their spiritual conflict. In each case, it has to be understood in its immediate context.

Being "in Christ" is one of the most reassuring truths for us to grasp as we seek to live for Him in an evil and hostile world. It is a key phrase expressing that He is the source and channel of all our blessings. At one time we were 'out of Christ', lost in our sins and on the way to eternal destruction, but through the grace of God and our faith in His Son, we are now secure in Him. At times the problems of life may assail us, but the unshakeable and unbreakable foundation of our faith remains: we are safe in Christ, eternally. And while it is true that we are associated with Him, it is equally true that we are incorporated into Him and as such we are one with Him.

No child of God needs to be a spiritual pauper.

1.4 - Chosen in Him

According as he hath chosen us in him before the foundation of the world, that we should be holy and without blame before him in love:

Those who are in Christ are God's chosen people. As such they are the objects of divine favour, the recipients of divine blessings, and the focus of divine purpose.

The "foundation of the world" is best understood to mean the creation and the beginning of time. It is referred to ten times in the New Testament. On three occasions, including this particular verse, the phrase is "before the foundation of the world" (Jn 17.24; Eph 1.4; 1 Pet 1.20). This emphasises the eternal nature of God's purposes. All other instances are prefixed by the words "since" or "from" and refer to an extended period following the creation.

We should note carefully that the choice presented here is not that of being chosen to be in Christ. It is not God choosing those who should be saved. Rather, it is God determining that those who are in Christ through faith should be the object of His favour and fulfil His purposes.

How did the Ephesians come to be in Christ? Further down the first chapter Paul reminds them of how it happened: they heard the gospel, believed it and trusted in Christ (Eph 1.13). They made the right choice. This has ever been God's simple way of receiving salvation, so simple that even a child can understand it.

What then are God's purposes for His own? Firstly, that they should be holy. This means that they are set apart for His glory, and their manner of life should reflect the holiness of God. Sinful habits will be abandoned, selfishness and waywardness will be resisted, and purity will be embraced. They will separate themselves from the evil of this world. This is an ongoing challenge for all of us.

Secondly, their manner of life should be blameless. To be blameless does not mean to be perfect. What it does mean is that there should be no contradictions in our lives that would leave us open to a justifiable charge of hypocrisy.

Thirdly, the underlying motive for believers must be to act out of love and devotion to God. In other words, they separate themselves unto God, to fulfil His will and to do whatever He commands them to do. It has been well said that 'separation from can breed Pharisees, whereas separation unto produces Nazarites'. Christ Himself perfectly manifested that He was chosen, holy, blameless, and motivated by love.

Take time to be holy.

23

1.5 - Adopted in Him

Having predestinated us unto the adoption of children by Jesus Christ to himself, according to the good pleasure of his will,

Two important words in this verse require us to adjust our thinking. God's predestination (or foreordination) does not refer to a place, either heaven or hell, as the eternal destiny that God has chosen for some. In fact, in all of the New Testament uses of the word the focus is on the specific purposes that God has for all of His children who have believed in Christ. In Romans 8.29-30, that purpose concerns us becoming like Christ by being conformed to the image of God's Son. In 1 Corinthians 2.7, where the word is translated "ordained", the eternal purpose is our glory. In Ephesians 1.5 the purpose is our adoption as sons, and in Ephesians 1.11-12 the purpose is not only our inheritance but also the praise of His glory.

The second adjustment requires us to understand that adoption is a special blessing of God for us. (The word 'sons' is to be preferred to 'children' in this verse, and the Bible truth should not be confused with current procedures of child adoption in society.) We become God's children by the new birth. We become God's sons by adoption. The first is focused on birth and entering the family; the second is focused on blessings and the privileges as full-grown sons in that family.

Only Paul uses the word 'adoption' in the New Testament; he does so here and on four other occasions. In Romans 8.15 our intimacy with God as our Father is in view. In Romans 8.23 the future redemption of the believer's body is the focus. In Romans 9.4 the historical privileges of the nation of Israel as God's 'son' are highlighted (cf. Ex 4.22). Finally, in Galatians 4.5-6, the redemptive work of Christ upon the cross is shown to have enabled us to receive adoption as the sons of God: "And because ye are sons, God hath sent forth the Spirit of his Son into your hearts, crying, Abba, Father." Reviewing this range of truth shows that both present and future blessings are included in our adoption and sonship.

God is not reluctant to make us His sons and to bless us abundantly. He has planned it so and it pleases Him to carry it out. The privileges of believers as sons carry with them corresponding responsibilities. We recall that King David had a wayward and rebellious son who broke his heart (2 Sam 18.33).

Children of the King should have the manners of the court.

1.6 - Accepted in Him

To the praise of the glory of his grace, wherein he hath made us accepted in the beloved.

These words are magnificent in their scope and at the same time infinitely tender in their expression. The verse begins with the first of three mentions in this chapter of divine purposes working out towards "the praise of his glory" (1.6, 12, 14). This is a reminder that if God is the source of the great drama of redemption for His creation, He is also its ultimate goal as the One to whom honour and worship are due. The glorious nature of His grace to us will be the theme of eternal praise. Indeed, His will, His pleasure, His grace, and His glory blend as one.

Our acceptance before God comes through our relationship with Christ, the beloved One. The Father and the Son share a mutual and eternal love. The Lord expressed this when He prayed to the Father before going to Calvary: "Father, I will that they also, whom thou hast given me, be with me where I am; that they may behold my glory, which thou hast given me: for thou lovedst me before the foundation of the world" (Jn 17.24). By that same love the Father has revealed to Christ "all things that himself doeth" and hath given "all things into his hand" (Jn 5.20; 3.35).

When we believe in Christ we are associated with Him, but more than that, we are incorporated into Him. His life becomes our life; His blessings become ours. We are accepted before God because of the acceptability of His Son. Christ pleased the Father in all things and completed His will, even to the death of the cross where He died alone and forsaken. (The only other New Testament use of the word for acceptance, in Lk 1.28, refers to Mary, the mother of Jesus, being "highly favoured".)

To be accepted is something that human hearts crave in their relationships one with the other. Families have been torn apart when certain members have felt neglected, disapproved of, or rejected. There are enough stories in the Bible itself to illustrate the tensions and strains that have arisen from favouritism and partiality in a family setting. The greater tragedy is that so many seem unconcerned about their need to get right with God and to be accepted by Him.

We do not need to wait for eternity to begin praising Him. Every day of our lives should begin and end with thankfulness to God. His undeserved favour lavished upon us should stir us to lift our hearts in wonder and worship.

Our acceptance before God is because of Christ,
whom this world rejected.

1.7 – Redeemed in Him

In whom we have redemption through his blood, the forgiveness of sins, according to the riches of his grace;

Paul enlarges on the many blessings that are to be found in Christ. The truth of redemption has its roots in the Old Testament history of Israel, particularly their period of cruel slavery in Egypt: "But because the Lord loved you ... the Lord brought you out with a mighty hand, and redeemed you out of the house of bondmen, from the hand of Pharaoh king of Egypt" (Deut 7.8). The last and most severe plague that God brought upon the land was the death of the firstborn; however, the Israelites were protected by the blood of the Passover lamb that was shed and applied to the doors of their homes (Ex 12.13).

Another relevant picture comes from New Testament times in the Roman Empire when household slaves were bought and sold like commodities in an open market. Sometimes personal freedom could be bought but at a high price. If we bring these two pictures together – one from the Jewish world and the other from the Gentile world – we see that the truth of redemption in biblical terms involves the shedding of blood as the necessary price to set a captive free. Slaves become sons!

Sinners are enslaved to Satan and can do nothing to procure their release. Their trespasses (the word used in this verse) are a result of them continually crossing the moral lines that a holy God has defined. God demanded a perfect sacrifice and the shedding of blood to atone for their sins. The writer to the Hebrews explained it like this: "And almost all things are by the law purged with blood; and without shedding of blood is no remission" (Heb 9.22). The apostle Peter wrote, "Forasmuch as ye know that ye were not redeemed with corruptible things, as silver and gold ... But with the precious blood of Christ, as of a lamb without blemish and without spot" (1 Pet 1.18-19). Here is God's remedy for man's ruin.

The liberation that Christ's redemption brings also means that sinners are released from the penalty of their sins. They can be fully forgiven because Another has borne the judgment and paid the price. The recurring phrase, "according to", directs us to the manner and measure in which the purposes of God are fulfilled as well as the motive (Eph 1.5, 7, 9, 11). Here the measure is immeasurable – "the riches of his grace".

Christ's redemption is free, full, and forever.

1. 8 - Enriched in Him

**Wherein he hath abounded toward us
in all wisdom and prudence;**

When God blesses out of the storehouses of His grace, He does so abundantly (the word could be translated 'superabounded', describing the great measure of His giving). He is not restrained or miserly, nor is He impoverished when He gives liberally out of His infinite resources. Those whom He blesses are all unworthy sinners, but on the principle of grace, they have received what they did not deserve.

That same rich grace bestows godly wisdom upon the child of God, wisdom he could never have apart from it. Godly wisdom is not to be equated with IQ or intellect. It refers to a spiritual understanding of what God has revealed in His Word. The paradox is that the universities of this world are filled with men and women of great intelligence who have not yet learned the ABCs of God's truth. Solomon asked God for such wisdom. His request pleased the Lord and it was granted (1 Kgs 3.9-10). The tragedy of his life was that he departed from the wisdom he had been given.

The prudence referred to can be regarded as the appropriate application of the wisdom that God gives to His children when they are instructed in His Word and guided by His Spirit. Those who are in Christ have a completely new way of thinking as well as new ways of speaking and acting: "Therefore if any man be in Christ, he is a new [creation]: old things are passed away; behold, all things are become new" (2 Cor 5.17). The discerning believer will begin to see things as God sees them and not be so easily deceived by appearances: "man looketh on the outward appearance but the Lord looketh on the heart" (1 Sam 16.7).

Just like the apostle Paul writing from a prison in Rome, John Bunyan wrote from a prison in Bedford where he spent twelve years (1660-1672). He aptly titled his autobiography *Grace Abounding to the Chief of Sinners*, combining two well-known verses: "But where sin abounded, grace did much more abound" (Rom 5.20), and "Christ Jesus came into the world to save sinners; of whom I am chief" (1 Tim 1.15). Bunyan wrote that 'It is profitable for Christians to be often calling to mind the very beginnings of grace within their souls.' We too may do so even now.

God is both gracious and generous with undeserving sinners.

1.9 - Instructed in Him

**Having made known unto us the mystery of his will,
according to his good pleasure
which he hath purposed in himself:**

Here is the first of the mysteries that are mentioned in Ephesians:

> the mystery of His will 1.9-10
> the mystery of Christ 3.3-4
> the mystery of the Church 3.9-10
> the mystery of 'the Bride' 5.32
> the mystery of the Gospel 6.19

Mysteries in the Bible are divine truths that had been previously hidden but are now revealed. Paul explained this to the Romans when he referred to preaching the gospel of Jesus Christ, "according to the revelation of the mystery, which was kept secret since the world began, but now is made manifest, and by the scriptures of the prophets, according to the commandment of the everlasting God, made known to all nations for the obedience of faith" (Rom 16.25-26). Some of the mysteries revealed in Ephesians are unique to the book; some overlap with other Scriptures.

The will of God is also a prominent theme in the first chapter of Ephesians (Eph 1.1, 5, 9, 11). His will is for His own pleasure (Eph 1.5). God is sovereign and He does not need to consult with mankind. However, as we are learning, God in grace has been pleased to reveal His will to us, not only in the details that should mould our personal lives before Him (Eph 5.17; 6.6), but also in the overarching grand design of His purposes for all creation. We have been instructed and let into 'God's sacred secrets'.

Adam and Eve were left in no doubt as to what God desired for them and expected of them (Gen 1.28; 2.15-17). After God had called Abram from Ur of the Chaldees, He had much to tell him also as to the divine plan for his promised seed. On another occasion, God said, "Shall I hide from Abraham that thing which I do; seeing that Abraham shall surely become a great and mighty nation, and all the nations of the earth shall be blessed in him?" (Gen 18.17-18). As a result of this God informed Abraham about the impending judgment on Sodom and Gomorrah. He is a God of revelation.

We are amazed at what God has revealed to us by His grace.

1.10 - Gathered Together in Him

That in the dispensation of the fulness of times he might gather together in one all things in Christ, both which are in heaven, and which are on earth; even in him:

Here is the eternal purpose, the mystery of His will (v. 9), that God has made known to us. It encompasses Christ and His creation and looks forward to a glorious consummation when Christ will be seen to be the Head of all things. In this respect Christ is not just the facilitator, He is the goal.

The dispensation of the fulness of times shows us that God's plans are carried out in God's time. We might say that He has a calendar and He has administered His creation in various ways down through the centuries. What still lies in the future is the universal acknowledgment that Christ is supreme. In this present age, Christ is absent from view and rejected by many. However, the millennial kingdom will see a complete change when the King will return in glory. Every knee shall bow and every tongue shall confess that Jesus Christ is Lord, to the glory of God the Father (Phil 2.10-11). This acknowledgment will encompass the heavens, the earth, and things under the earth – the celestial, the terrestrial and the infernal (those in hades awaiting their eternal fate). In other words, all of creation will bow down to Him. The Old Testament story of Joseph prefigures the honour that the rejected son receives (Gen 42.6). The difference though was that Joseph's brothers confessed their wrongdoing and were reconciled to him before it was too late.

This verse is not teaching universal salvation but a final and universal admission of that which has always been true – Christ is supreme! Those who rejected and crucified Him will see Him again. Their last view of Him had been of an apparently helpless victim expiring upon a cross in shame and defeat. But the brightness of His glory, majesty and power will be overwhelming when they next see Him. Those of earth who refused His mercy and grace will weep and wail because of Him (Rev 1.7). They will realise that having refused God's Son and His great salvation, there is nothing ahead of them except eternal judgment.

Once we are in Christ, we are in Him forever.

1.11 – Entitled in Him

In whom also we have obtained an inheritance, being predestinated according to the purpose of him who worketh all things after the counsel of his own will:

There is no end to the blessings in Christ. We can enter into the good of them now, but eternity will be an ongoing revelation and enjoyment of them all in full measure. Our spiritual riches put the ascribed wealth of earth's billionaires in the shade. And of course, the rich men of the earth must leave all of their wealth behind. The famous treasures left in the tomb of Tutankhamun, an Egyptian pharaoh, were meant to accompany and sustain him in the afterlife. Thousands of years later, when his tomb was uncovered, they were still there! The child of God knows that the best is yet to come. We are heirs of God and joint-heirs with Christ (Rom 8.17), with a future inheritance reserved in heaven for us (1 Pet 1.4).

There are parallels between the letter to the Ephesians and the book of

Joshua. After 40 years of wandering in the wilderness under Moses, the children of Israel entered Canaan, the promised land, under Joshua. Their blessings were not automatically enjoyed; they were appropriated through warfare (cf. Eph 6.10-18). What is disappointing to note is that after the land was conquered, seven tribes were slow to claim their inheritance. Joshua was perplexed: "How long are ye slack to go to possess the land, which the Lord God of your fathers hath given you?" (Josh 18.3). Perhaps the same could be same of some of us who behave as spiritual paupers instead of enjoying the riches of His grace day by day.

As we have noted already, God in eternity planned it so that His children would be spiritually wealthy. He has been working out His eternal purposes in time and through history according to His will. Furthermore, these purposes are always according to His character, and He is unchanging in His goodness, mercy and grace. He wants the best for all of us. When we were in our sins He loved us. Now, having become His children through faith in Christ, He loves us still, even when we stumble on the pathway of life. He knows we are a work in progress, but He will perfect that which concerns us (Ps 138.8; Phil 1.6). The next verse will show the bigger picture.

All of God's children are spiritual millionaires.

1.12 - Trusting in Him

**That we should be to the praise of his glory,
who first trusted in Christ.**

Once again the ultimate reason for God blessing us goes far beyond ourselves. Our lives should result in Him being praised and glorified. It is not that we are of secondary importance, merely a means to an end. We recall that it was for us that God gave His Son and Christ gave His all, but in the grand scheme of things we understand that eternal praise should redound to His Name.

Paul's use of the pronoun 'we' in this verse, 'you' in verse 13, and 'our' in verse 14, indicates a progression in keeping with the early history of the Church. Perhaps he is thinking firstly of Christians who had once been Jews, then in verse 13 of the predominantly Gentile background of the Ephesian believers, before he brings it all together in verse 14 and speaks of common blessings in Christ.

The word 'trusted' in this verse carries the thought of hoping. Down through the centuries until Christ came, the Jews had kept alive the hope of a coming Messiah. When they heard the gospel, the challenge for them was to recognise that Jesus of Nazareth was the Christ, God's Anointed. In His day Christ's claims were rejected by the nation at large and they eventually had Him crucified. However, following His death and resurrection, the disciples were invigorated to spread the gospel message widely. Many Jews still resisted the truth of the gospel. Saul of Tarsus was not only violently opposed to it, but he also sought to put an end to the propagation of the message. By God's grace Saul was converted on the Damascus Road and his life was transformed. He became the torchbearer of the light of the gospel and he shone brightly wherever he was.

When Paul came to Ephesus on his second missionary journey, he began in his customary fashion by preaching first in the synagogue to the Jews. After three months the response was so negative and antagonistic that he left the synagogue and used "the school of one Tyrannus" as his base. For another two years the gospel was faithfully and widely proclaimed so that everyone in the region "heard the word of the Lord Jesus, both Jews and Greeks" (Acts 19.10). Many Gentiles turned from their dead and false idols to serve the living and true God, and despite much opposition, the church at Ephesus grew.

Praising God is never a waste of time.

1.13 – The Seal of the Spirit

In whom ye also trusted, after that ye heard the word of truth, the gospel of your salvation: in whom also after that ye believed, ye were sealed with that holy Spirit of promise,

The Ephesians who had been Gentiles had also heard the gospel and believed it. Even though the word 'trusted' is not in the original text, it is certainly implied. They possessed full salvation, just like the converts from Judaism, through faith alone in Christ alone. This is important to remember – regarding spiritual blessedness, God is no respecter of persons (Acts 10.34). There is not one of His children who is second-rate in His sight.

'Upon believing', as the original words mean, rather than some time afterwards, they were sealed with the Holy Spirit. At the moment of conversion, the Holy Spirit of God comes to permanently indwell the new believer. This was the promise of Christ when He addressed His disciples in the upper room. He was anticipating His departure from them by way of His death upon the cross, but He promised them a Comforter just like Himself. That Comforter was the Holy Spirit: "And I will pray the Father, and he shall give you another Comforter, that he may abide with you for ever; even the Spirit of truth; whom the world cannot receive, because it seeth him not, neither knoweth him: but ye know him; for he dwelleth with you, and shall be in you" (Jn 14.16-17).

The indwelling Holy Spirit is the definitive mark of divine ownership: "But ye are not in the flesh, but in the Spirit, if so be that the Spirit of God dwell in you. Now if any man have not the Spirit of Christ, he is none of his" (Rom 8.9). We do not need to wait for Him or pray for Him to indwell us. Charismatic confusion has caused some to believe that following conversion they must experience 'the baptism of the Spirit', a higher blessing that is demonstrated by the ability to speak in tongues. This conclusion comes from a misunderstanding of the unique historical event that took place on the day of Pentecost (Acts 2). The Holy Spirit also reassures us that we belong to Christ: "The

Spirit itself beareth witness with our spirit, that we are the children of God" (Rom 8.16).

God's seal of ownership will never be broken.

1.14 – The Guarantee of the Spirit

Which is the earnest of our inheritance until the redemption of the purchased possession, unto the praise of his glory.

The Holy Spirit dwelling within us is not only the permanent mark of divine ownership but also the guarantee, or pledge, of the blessings that are yet to come. He is like the firstfruits of a forthcoming bountiful harvest. Even though we enjoy heavenly blessings now, these will be known in all their fulness in the future.

One example of this is the matter of redemption. The purchase price was paid in blood to set us free; we now belong to Christ and serve Him as our master. These are the past and present aspects of our redemption; however, the redemption of our bodies – us being glorified and fitted for heaven – has not yet taken place. These bodies are prone to increasing weakness and degeneration as we grow older, and so they would never be suited to heaven. Not only that but the flesh, our sinful nature, is still active and will seek to express itself through these mortal bodies. That is why the truth of a bodily resurrection is so important. Our future inheritance will include us acquiring bodies of glory: "And not only they, but ourselves also, which have the firstfruits of the Spirit, even we ourselves groan within ourselves, waiting for the adoption, to wit, the redemption of our body" (Rom 8.23).

In writing to the Corinthians, Paul anticipated the bodily resurrection of believers: "For we that are in this tabernacle do groan, being burdened: not for that we would be unclothed, but clothed upon, that mortality might be swallowed up of life. Now he that hath wrought us for the selfsame thing is God, who also hath given us the earnest of the Spirit" (2 Cor 5.4-5). Once again, the Holy Spirit is shown to be the guarantor of this promise.

Glorified bodies, immortal and free from any taint of sin, will be perfectly suited to the heavenly realm. We will never become tired, or feel an ache or pain again. Many Christians are sorely afflicted by chronic illness and each day for them is a severe trial. What a glorious prospect is theirs that one day they will be free from all of their present suffering. Here are more reasons to praise our God and give Him glory.

For the child of God, the best is yet to be.

1.15 - A Good Report

Wherefore I also, after I heard of your faith in the Lord Jesus, and love unto all the saints,

One can sense Paul's delight in receiving a good report about these Christians. This meant that others had faithfully conveyed a positive report to him, whether in a formal way or just in casual conversation. Paul would probably have enquired of friends who had visited Ephesus as to the welfare of the believers. Whatever way he came about the news, there was a mutual pleasure in knowing that the Ephesian Christians were making progress.

At times it seems that only bad news travels fast. It is often biased and focused on the failings of others. It can so quickly descend to the level of malicious gossip and corrupt the minds and hearts of both messenger and recipient alike. Paul would not have indulged in this type of conversation, but on occasions when the news was not so good, he addressed the problems firmly but fairly (1 Cor 1.11).

There is always joy when men, women and younger folk come to faith in Christ. What is even more encouraging is to see the new converts making progress, growing in grace and in the knowledge of the Lord Jesus Christ. Paul revelled in this.

"Your faith" would relate to their continuance in both the doctrine and practices they had been taught. They were surrounded by all the familiar trappings of idolatry and immorality; temptation was never far away. There would still have been opposition from the general population among whom they lived.

Their love was expressed to all the saints. That is not as easy as it sounds because we must confess that we are often partial in this matter. We love those who seem to love us and think and act as we do. We tend to avoid mingling too much with others that we feel are not quite our type, or not up to our standard. At times we have been rebuked in our spirits to come across someone who genuinely cares for all of God's people (2 Cor 11.28). The Ephesian believers had given ample evidence that they truly loved one another. Paul would later encourage them to continue in the same, and no doubt this would have been demonstrated in practical ways. It was no mere profession.

"As cold waters to a thirsty soul,
so is good news from a far country." (Prov 25.25)

1.16 - Praise and Prayer

Cease not to give thanks for you,
making mention of you in my prayers;

One of the characteristics of Paul's life was his habit of praying. It marked him out from his first days as a Christian. A man called Ananias was directed by the Lord to go and assist the new convert, then known as Saul of Tarsus. Precise details were given as to the right street, the right house, and the right person. Ananias was told how he could identify Saul – he would find him praying (Acts 9.11).

When Paul wrote to the Ephesians of his unceasing remembrance and thanksgiving, he was not exaggerating. He frequently remembered them all before the throne of grace, but not just them: he told the Romans, the Colossians, and the Thessalonians the same (Rom 1.9; Col 1.9; 1 Thess 1.3; 2.13). How must Timothy have felt when Paul wrote in his last letter to him: "I thank God ... that without ceasing I have remembrance of thee in my prayers night and day" (2 Tim 1.3)? What an encouragement!

Paul likely knew many of the believers in Ephesus by name and these would have been mentioned specifically in his praise and prayer. His knowledge of individuals and his interest in them is illustrated in the last chapter of his letter to the Romans where he listed many different people and their particular contribution to the work of God. His prayer requests were also specific, as we shall see in the two prayers in this letter. Sometimes our prayers are so vague that it would be difficult to know if they were ever answered.

Paul's good advice, "Pray without ceasing" (1 Thess 5.17), echoes down through the centuries. Our personal prayer lives are a measure of our spiritual health. The time we spend alone with God in private and the earnestness with which we lay hold upon Him are sure indicators of our commitment to Him. In the same way, the public prayer meeting in the local assembly reflects the spiritual temperature of the church. Why is it so often the worst attended meeting? Praising and praying are never a waste of time. It is good to lead with the first before resorting to the second, so that we give thanks to God before making our requests. When we do so with fervency and sincerity, God is honoured, Christ is exalted, others are blessed, and we are kept in tune.

Praise and prayer are twins; keep them together.

1.17 - Endowment

**That the God of our Lord Jesus Christ, the Father of glory,
may give unto you the spirit of wisdom and revelation
in the knowledge of him:**

Paul is now framing his prayer requests for the Ephesian believers. "The God of our Lord Jesus Christ" is a unique expression reminding us of Christ's dependent humanity. It is also unusual for Paul to refer to God as "the Father of glory" but this beautiful name is only one of several special titles that are linked to the Fatherhood of God. In the New Testament, He is also described as the Father of mercies, the Father of all, the Father of spirits, and the Father of lights (2 Cor 1.3; Eph 4.6; Heb 12.9; Jas 1.17). The Father is also mentioned frequently in relation to His Son, the Lord Jesus Christ.

Wisdom in this context means spiritual understanding. God is its source and it is only He who can endow us with it (Jas 1.5). Revelation means that God Himself unveils more and more of His glory and majesty to us. Together these blessings enable us to make progress and get to know God better. This indicates a full knowledge rather than an elementary and patchy kind of acquaintance with Him. Paul expressed a similar request in his letter to the Philippians: "That I may know him, and the power of his resurrection, and the fellowship of his sufferings, being made conformable unto his death" (Phil 3.10). For one who knew the Lord so well it was not enough; he longed to know Him better.

Acquiring this knowledge is a vital process in our Christian experience because we do not stand still as far as spiritual things are concerned: we are either going forward or we are slipping backwards. Then again, it is more than factual knowledge; it is the growing knowledge of a deepening personal relationship with God. This is what makes Christianity real and truly amazing: we weak and mortal creatures can enjoy daily communion with the almighty and eternal God.

We have noted that each believer is indwelt by the Spirit of God. Perhaps what is indicated in this verse is that the Holy Spirit guides and directs our human spirits to appreciate these blessings. Wisdom and revelation lead us into a deeper knowledge, and in return, that deeper knowledge opens up for us more wisdom and understanding.

Glory begins and ends with God.

1.18 - Enlightenment

The eyes of your understanding be enlightened; that ye may know what is the hope of his calling, and what the riches of the glory of his inheritance in the saints,

Paul's desire for his friends included a deeper knowledge of God Himself, and also an understanding of what He is doing. This would require 'the eyes of your heart', as the original reads, to be enlightened. Mind and heart, intellect and emotions, are so intertwined that it is not always possible to separate them. In Scripture, the use of the word 'heart' often includes the moral and spiritual character of our inner beings, including our mind and will.

Students of history define 'the Enlightenment' as a period of European history in the 17th and 18th centuries in which great advances were made in human philosophy, politics and science. It was claimed that primitive belief in God and adherence to religious superstition would only hinder human progress and should be discarded. Man's intellectual powers and reasoning would usher in an age of utopian bliss. This proud and arrogant tenet is widely accepted today, despite all evidence to the contrary. After two world wars in the last century alone, man's inhumanity to man seems only to be increasing. One must wonder what the humanistic definition of progress is?

Hope for the Christian is full of the assurance that the Lord will fulfil His promises, and that which we have been called to will be finally realised. Future blessings will include the certainty of the Lord's return, the transformation of the living saints, the resurrection of sleeping saints, the glory of heaven, and the joy of being with Christ and like Him forever. There will be no more sorrow or pain, and no more tears or bereavement. Our glorified bodies and minds will never degenerate or know tiredness and weakness again. There will also be no more struggle with sin and the flesh; these will have no place in us or in heaven.

While it is true that the saints, those separated unto the Lord, will be His inheritance, perhaps in context the preferred thought is that of the blessings we shall receive as our inheritance. God's riches are incalculable and truly glorious. Originally the word for inheritance referred to a portion assigned by lot. There was an element of chance in a random selection procedure. This is not the case with our inheritance. God finely tunes His blessings to meet our individual needs as well as our common needs.

Only Christ, the Light of the world,
can dispel the darkness in men's hearts.

1.19 - Enablement

And what is the exceeding greatness of his power to us-ward who believe, according to the working of his mighty power,

Enlightened, enriched and enabled! Knowledge, hope, riches, and now power are ours. We are climbing higher as Paul envisages even greater blessings. Believers often feel weak, not only physically and mentally but also spiritually. Here is a reminder of divine omnipotence at our disposal. Paul's language spills forth in a profusion of words that are so closely related that it is not easy to distinguish them. The overall effect is to reassure us and then challenge us so that we will learn to appropriate these divine gifts.

The dynamic power of God is described as being both great and abundant in its quality and quantity. Paul will use the same word again

(Eph 1.21; 3.7, 16, 20). This power can only be known by those who have believed in Christ and who continue to walk by faith. It is available at all times, in every place, and under all circumstances. There are no power cuts on God's side.

God's power has always been at work. It has been manifested down through the centuries of earth's history, if only men had the eyes to see it. Creation came into being by the word of His power. As far as earth is concerned, divine power maintains this planet and keeps it at just the right distance from the sun. Any deviation in this would have us either frozen or scorched to death. Biblical history is a revelation of God's power as seen in Israel's redemption from Egypt and through the Red Sea, the nation's preservation in the wilderness and their conquest of the land.

In the life of the Lord Jesus Christ, divine power was revealed in many wonderful ways including feeding thousands, calming storms, healing the sick, and raising the dead. After Christ changed the water into wine at a wedding, the apostle John wrote: "This beginning of miracles did Jesus in Cana of Galilee, and manifested his glory; and his disciples believed on him" (Jn 2.11). These powerful miracles, or 'signs' as John called them, were recorded so that people might believe that Jesus was the Christ, the Son of God, and that through believing they might have life through His Name (Jn 20.30-31).

Weak as we are, we are in touch with the Omnipotent.

1.20 - Resurrection Power

Which he wrought in Christ, when he raised him from the dead, and set him at his own right hand in the heavenly places,

Here then is the great demonstration of God's power in the resurrection of Christ. Nothing could withstand it. No satanic opposition, no human scheming, and no military might could resist the almighty power of God in raising His Son from the grave. Christ had told His disciples on three occasions that the Son of Man must rise again after a cruel death, but they were slow to understand and found it hard to take in, even when they heard reports that He had been seen. Paradoxically, the enemies of Christ were not slow at all to consider the possibility of resurrection. They tried to take all precautions to prevent it but were quick to believe it, even bribing people to say that the disciples had stolen the body and taken it away.

God's claims had been met at Calvary: all that His justice demanded had been exacted, and the penalty of sin had been paid in full. The perfect sacrifice was accepted. After the Lord rose from the dead He appeared unto His own for forty days. At least ten post-resurrection appearances are recorded. It was from the Mount of Olives that He ascended from earth and into heaven itself.

Other scriptures give us the full picture. God the Father raised Him (Eph 1.20); Christ, the Son, took up His own life again (Jn 2.19; 10.17-18); and the Spirit of God was also instrumental in the Saviour's resurrection (Rom 8.11).

He was taken up (Acts 1.9); He went up (Acts 1.10); He ascended up on high (Eph 4.8); He was carried up (Lk 24.51); and He was received up (Mk 16.19). He passed through the heavens (Heb 4.14) and ascended up far above all the heavens (Eph 4.10); He entered into heaven itself (Heb 9.24) and was made higher than the heavens (Heb 7.26). God set Him down (Eph 1.20) and He set Himself down (Heb 1.3) on the right hand of God (1 Pet 3.22) and of the throne of the Majesty in the heavens (Heb 8.1).

Today the Lord Jesus Christ appears in heaven for us as our Great High Priest. We are exhorted to come boldly before His throne of grace in every time of need (Heb 4.16).

Christ's resurrection assures our resurrection.

1.21 – Far Above All

**Far above all principality, and power,
and might, and dominion, and every name that is named,
not only in this world, but also in that which is to come:**

When Christ came to earth, He could only move downwards because He already occupied the highest place in heaven. In Philippians 2 we read of the voluntary self-humbling of the Son of God and His seven downward steps, right down to the death of the cross. Having completed the wonderful work of salvation at Calvary, and having completely satisfied the claims of justice, "God also hath highly exalted him, and given him a name which is above every name: that at the name of Jesus every knee should bow, of things in heaven, and things in earth, and things under the earth; and that every tongue should confess that Jesus Christ is Lord, to the glory of God the Father" (Phil 2.9-11). A risen Man is far above all, and His Name excels every other name.

The four similar words in this verse relate to the rule, authority, power, and dominion of both men and angels, upon the earth and in the unseen spirit world above. The devil and his angels continue seeking to oppose Christ and His people. They presently exert great influence and hold sway over many lives down here upon earth, but in a future day, their total defeat will be manifested for all to see.

Christ's exalted position is far above all; this refers to His dignity as much as any thought of a location. All things were created by Him and for Him (Col 1.16) and the Father has put all things in subjection under Him: "For he hath put all things under his feet ... and when all things shall be subdued unto him, then shall the Son also himself be subject unto him that put all things under him, that God may be all in all" (1 Cor 15.27-28). Christ will willingly hand over the kingdom to the Father: "Then cometh the end, when he shall have delivered up the kingdom to God, even the Father; when he shall have put down all rule and all authority and power" (1 Cor 15.24).

Far above all, far above all,
God has exalted Him far above all;
Thrones and dominions before Him shall fall
But Jesus my Saviour is far above all.

1.22 - Head Over All

And hath put all things under his feet,
and gave him to be the head over all things to the church,

We are climbing yet higher. From a consideration of Christ's exaltation above His enemies, we are now directed to His headship over those who love Him because He first loved them. All this and more are contained in Paul's prayer.

It was His enemies who nailed His feet to a cross. It was His friends, the faithful believing women, who after His resurrection held Him by the feet and worshipped Him (Mt 28.9). Their hearts were filled with joyful wonder at seeing Him again. During His earthly ministry, Mary of Bethany had sat at His feet to learn, had fallen at His feet to plead, and had bowed at His feet to worship. Having anointed Him with precious ointment, she wiped His feet with her hair; that day the house was filled with the beautiful fragrance (Jn 12.3).

When Christ ascended to heaven from the Mount of Olives, the disciples were reminded by the angels that He would return in like manner. Indeed, a prophetic reference to Christ's return in majestic glory promises the same: "And his feet shall stand in that day upon the mount of Olives, which is before Jerusalem on the east" (Zech 14.4).

The "all things" are significant in Ephesians. There are no half measures with God. His purposes are viewed as a vast panorama, so that if all things are to be gathered together in Christ (Eph 1.10), and God is working all things according to the counsel of His own will (Eph 1.11), then all things – friend or foe – must be put under Him.

The references to "the church" in Ephesians go beyond the reality of a local group of Christians in Ephesus or elsewhere. The Church here includes every believer in Christ from the day of Pentecost until the Rapture. This first reference paves the way for fresh revelation as to the composition, character and destiny of the Church. Here the headship of Christ is stated: Christ is supreme and those who have come to believe in Him owe their total allegiance to Him.

It is a good thing to spend time at Christ's feet every day.

1.23 - Filling All

Which is his body, the fulness of him that filleth all in all.

The Church is described for the first time as the body of Christ. This truth was revealed to the apostle Paul and in his various writings, he expands it in different ways. Christ has been identified as the Head; all believers constitute His body. This represents perfect union and completeness. Christ's life is the same life that flows through the body. He continuously makes available all that the body requires so that it lacks nothing to function properly. It obeys His will and honours Him in all things.

In Paul's second prayer in this letter, he desired that the believers would be filled "with all the fulness of God" (Eph 3.19). In terms of their maturity, he went on to speak of them growing into the stature of "the fulness of Christ" (Eph 4.13). Finally, he instructed them to be filled "with the Spirit" (Eph 5.18). The three Persons of the Godhead – the Father, Son, and Holy Spirit – are interested in us so that we might truly be full of all that is godly, Christlike and spiritual. After their conversion, some of the Ephesians might have experienced poverty and emptiness. In Christ, however, they could enjoy spiritual prosperity and fulness.

The world is obsessed with the material and the temporal. People chase after fulfilment and satisfaction, hoping to find them in pleasure and riches, yet these elude them. Solomon was in a position to try all that the world could offer to satisfy the soul, and yet at the end, he could only conclude that it was empty and in vain (Eccl 12.8). There have been those who boasted of their godlessness, but when they came to face death and eternity, they realised that they were left with nothing and had no hope.

Christ Himself fills the the "all in all" of the universe. This has not yet been manifested to the world at large. Presently, like David was when Absalom revolted against him and usurped the throne, Christ is an absent King in rejection. He is exalted in heaven and in the hearts of His own as their King, but to many of the unbelieving upon the earth He is still the despised Nazarene.

To live with Christ is to enjoy His fulness;
to live without Him is to experience emptiness.

Chapter 2

Nearness in Christ

Paul reminds the Ephesians that they were once spiritually dead in their sins, but are now made alive and lifted up through God's saving grace. He also reminds the Gentile believers of how far away they were from God, but are now brought near to be equally one with Jewish believers in God's family.

2.1 - Dead

**And you hath he quickened,
who were dead in trespasses and sins;**

Beginning another long sentence (vv. 1-7), Paul reminded the Ephesians of their former state. He did this to magnify the grace of God and to show in fuller measure the greatness of the work God had accomplished in them. It is useful for believers to reflect on their past: what they were in their sins, where they were going in terms of their destiny, and how hopeless they were, being unable to help themselves.

To be dead in trespasses and sins means to be devoid of spiritual life and separated from God, the source of life. It does not mean that we cannot think or choose to act in a particular way, nor does it mean that we cannot respond to the voice of God. However, it does mean that we cannot do anything to save ourselves.

Trespasses indicate crossing a line that God has drawn. We are all familiar with the signs on the fences of certain government installations or private properties: 'Trespassers will be prosecuted'. In other words, if we breach the fence by climbing over it or breaking through it, and are found on the wrong side, we are liable to be arrested and charged with an offence. In the ten commandments given through Moses, God drew clear lines of demarcation. If God has said "Thou shalt not steal", then taking something that is not one's own shows a disregard for His command and leaves one guilty. The same applies to all of the other commandments.

Sinning carries the thought of missing the mark and failing to reach the standard that God has set. This is the exact idea represented by the well-known gospel verse diagnosing the human condition: "For all have sinned, and come short of the glory of God" (Rom 3.23). There are sins of commission when we do what we should not do. There are also sins of omission when we fail to do what we should do. There are sins of thought, word, and deed. The nature we have inherited from our first parents, Adam and Eve, means not only that we were born in sin but

51

also, we practice sin. God's eternal judgment will not be because of a man's nature but because of his deeds or 'works' (Rev 20.12-13)

It is God alone who can make the dead sinner live. The same power that raised Christ from the dead operates in the one who believes in Christ and thereby receives eternal life.

God's gift of eternal life is offered to all.

2.2 - *Dominated*

Wherein in time past ye walked according to the course of this world, according to the prince of the power of the air, the spirit that now worketh in the children of disobedience:

The time markers throughout the letter are full of interest. As mentioned earlier, the purposes of God stretch from the eternal past to the eternal future. His great plan began "before the foundation of the world" and will continue to "the fulness of times" (Eph 1.4, 10). Even within the short span of our own lives upon this earth we have our past, as mentioned in this verse, but we look forward to "the ages to come" (Eph 2.7).

Dead men walking? Yes, before coming to Christ they lived worldly lives. All of their thoughts and attitudes, desires and ambitions, principles and practices were godless. The world continues in this way today with men and women following after temporal and material things; they think only in terms of the here and now. Many consider that God is dead, and so they can live and do as they like. They sin with impunity. They boast that humanity is making progress, all the more so for having cast off 'primitive religion and superstition', as they might say. They have not stopped to think of the road they are travelling and their final destination.

The prince of the power of the air is another name for Satan. He is also described as "the god of this world" (2 Cor 4.4). He exerts his evil influence in the spirit world above and physical world here below.

While it is true that Christ defeated him at Calvary, he remains active and works overtime, as it were, to frustrate God's purposes and hinder God's people. He knows he is living on borrowed time because one day he will be consigned to the lake of fire forever (Rev 20.10). Satan is not omnipresent but those angels who sinned with him continue to do his bidding throughout the world.

Despite all claims to the contrary, unbelievers are not free at all. They are slaves of a cruel master who controls them. They obey the devil rather than obeying God. Satan's first approach to Eve in the Garden of Eden caused her to doubt God's word, disregard His warning, and disobey His command. He continues to work in this way today.

Mankind cannot make real progress if it is travelling in the wrong direction.

2.3 - Destined for Wrath

Among whom also we all had our conversation in times past in the lusts of our flesh, fulfilling the desires of the flesh and of the mind; and were by nature the children of wrath, even as others.

Paul includes himself when he speaks of the former way of living, as the word 'conversation' means in the New Testament. (It does not refer to our speech.) Perhaps again he is including those of Jewish descent and showing that in terms of sinful behaviour, nothing separated them from the Gentiles.

"The lusts of the flesh" and "the desires of the flesh and of the mind" are general terms encompassing all evil and rebellious desires. (God's desires, or "will", in chapter 1.5, 9, 11 are all holy and for our blessing.) These sinful desires are not restricted to sexual impurity; they would include the desire for pleasure, possessions, or position. In this context "the flesh" refers to the carnal nature that all of us were born with; it manifests itself in self-indulgence and sinful deeds. Little has changed in the history of mankind so that pride, selfishness, jealousy, and envy are just as prevalent today as they ever were. A sinful nature produces sinful behaviour.

All actions have consequences, and here the judgment of God is implied. A holy God is righteously angry against sin and the Scriptures always spell out the results of sin. God warns before He judges: Adam and Eve were told that to eat from the forbidden tree would bring death. The Israelites were told that to forsake their God and follow after idols would bring judgment, and to disregard God's word would bring a curse. It is no different in this present day – the wages of sin is death (Rom 6.23). Some disregard God's warnings and live as if there will never be a day of reckoning. This does not in any way change the diagnosis of man's sinful condition, and the prognosis concerning the outcome.

God's anger is His fixed disposition against all that is sinful. His unchanging holiness means His unchanging pleasure in that which is good, and His unchanging displeasure with that which is evil. His anger is never, as some would portray it in human terms, a sudden lashing out in uncontrolled violence and hatred. There is a sense in which the character of the eternal God is predictable when it comes to His judgment upon sin. There are no surprises. By contrast, His grace and goodness are so often more than we could ever imagine!

A self-indulgent life is a waste.

2.4 - God Has Made The Difference

But God, who is rich in mercy, for his great love wherewith he loved us,

One cannot read the opening words of this verse without feeling a sense of wonder. The words "but God", make all the difference. God has taken the initiative in the matter of salvation because He is a God of mercy and love.

The situation for us sinners was perilous and hopeless. We were dead in our sins before a living God, dominated by a cruel master before a jealous God, disobedient before a holy God, and destined for eternal judgment before a righteous God.

But God is also merciful. He is infinitely rich in this regard. His mercy is full (Jas 3.17) and abundant (1 Pet 1.3). Other scriptures describe His mercy as being great (Num 14.19) and enduring forever (Ps 118.1, 29). He delights in mercy, (Mic 7.18) and expresses it in tenderness (Lk 1.78).

Grace has been described as God blessing us with what we do not deserve, and mercy as God withholding from us what do deserve. In other words, because of God's mercy we are spared His judgment. While this summary might be helpful in a measure, it does not do justice to the breadth of meaning in the word 'mercy'. The positive aspects of mercy include God's pity and compassion upon sinners, bringing relief to them in their desperate need.

The greatness of God's love has also been extended to lost sinners. Divine love is the reason for His mercy. He acts to satisfy His heart of love. Once again it is clear that God is bountiful and unsparing in His desire to bless sinners. We are transported to a realm of no limits where we can only wonder and worship. All of God's attributes are infinite, just as He is. We do God no justice when we reduce His dealings with mankind to neat formulae. Should we ever come to a point that we think we understand Him and His ways, we can be sure we are still paddling on the brink of a vast ocean of truth. We have only just begun!

His love is all the more amazing when we recall that it is all-inclusive. God loves a world of sinners and He has proved it in the giving of His only and well-beloved Son to the death of a cross.

God's children are enveloped in His love.

2.5 - Alive in Christ

**Even when we were dead in sins,
hath quickened us together with Christ, (by grace ye are saved;)**

The extent of the sinner's helplessness is emphasised again: it is to be spiritually dead before a living God. The original word used here refers to transgressions: sinners have gone beyond the limits that God has set and crossed the lines that He has demarcated.

The quickening power of God in raising Christ from the dead is the same power that brings life to dead sinners. The believer is linked with Christ in His death, burial, and resurrection. This truth is expanded in Romans 6.4: "Therefore we are buried with him by baptism into death: that like as Christ was raised up from the dead by the glory of the Father, even so we also should walk in newness of life." The practical implication of this is that believers should exhibit a transformed lifestyle. All of the prepositions showing our relationship to Christ and the subsequent blessings we enjoy are full of meaning: "in Christ" (Eph 1.3) – incorporation; "with Christ" (Eph 2.5) – association; "unto Christ" (Eph 5.24) – devotion; "from Christ" (Eph 1.2) – the source; "by Christ" (Eph 3.9) – the means; "through Christ" (Eph 2.7) – the channel.

Mercy, love, and grace form a lovely triad of blessings. The principle of God's grace always exceeds human computation, going far beyond what we can conceive or imagine. Using worldly logic, it does not make sense. Justice would demand that transgressors be punished, but because of God's grace, the transgressor can go free. It is one thing to have guilt removed; it is quite another to be elevated to heights of blessedness. All of God's blessings have come to us because of our association with His Son, the Lord Jesus Christ.

Salvation implies being rescued from a place of danger and being transferred to a place of security. Before believing in Christ, sinners were travelling on a downward road. The Scriptures are clear in revealing that their destiny was hell and the lake of fire forever. It is important for us to remember this. We need to remember that on the cross the Saviour bore the punishment for all our sins. From out of the darkness the cry was heard: "Finished!"

How good it is to be safe in Christ.

2. 6 - Seated with Christ

And hath raised us up together, and made us sit together in heavenly places in Christ Jesus:

Total identification with Christ in His resurrection, ascension and exaltation are the blessings that believers have received. To enjoy the full benefit of these truths requires us to appreciate and appropriate them in our daily living. Having died with Christ implies that the old life was left behind; being raised with Christ means that a new life has begun.

The force of the words indicates our oneness with Christ rather than our closeness. We are not regarded as being adjacent but as being one together. This is an intimate and unbreakable union. It was planned in eternity past, forged in the present, and will endure for all eternity to come.

One parallel passage in Paul's letter to the Colossians (there are many such correspondences between the two letters) states that believers have been "buried with him in baptism, wherein also ye are risen with him through the faith of the operation of God, who hath raised him from the dead. And you, being dead in your sins ... hath he quickened together with him, having forgiven you all trespasses" (Col 2.12-13).

God has granted us oneness with Christ in His exaltation to God's right hand. Day by day this truth can fortify us so that while we are here physically upon the earth, we can revel and rejoice in knowing that our true place is presently not so much with Him (that is yet to come), but in Him. We are welcome before that heavenly throne and in times of need we should boldly resort there in prayer, to obtain mercy and find grace to help (Heb 4.16).

Once again the reference to 'heavenly places' must be interpreted in its immediate context. Here it is linked with Christ and where He is, in the place of honour and majesty at God's right hand. Our thoughts and aspirations should be there. We are strangers and pilgrims here on this earth, but we are heading home. Again Paul encouraged the Colossians "to seek those things which are above, where Christ sitteth on the right hand of God. Set your affection on things above, not on things on the earth" (Col 3.1-2).

Heavenly blessings can be enjoyed here and now.

2. 7 - God's Kindness

That in the ages to come he might shew the exceeding riches of his grace in his kindness toward us through Christ Jesus.

The purposes of God are seen to reach far into the future. The "ages to come" include eternal ages that cannot be easily defined or even fully understood.

This is a verse with superlatives. The meaning of the word 'exceeding' has the idea of throwing beyond. It takes us back to the ancient Greek games where athletes competed in using the javelin, each trying to out-throw the other. In modern times the world javelin record belongs to a Czech athlete, Jan Železný. In 1996, in the German city of Jena, he achieved a throw of 98.48 metres. While this record has stood for many years, one day it will likely be broken.

When God's grace and kindness go on display, there will be none to equal or surpass them. The generous philanthropists of this world are to be commended in giving away billions out of their fortunes to assist the needy of this world. However, none has ever willingly given up an only son to a cruel death so that others might be blessed. Upon the cross of Calvary, the greatest price was paid that the greatest blessing might be enjoyed by us undeserving sinners. God gave His Son and Christ Jesus gave His all. No sacrifice was ever greater.

In the coming ages, God will put on display the superabundant riches of His grace and kindness. He will do so for His glory and praise. His great kindness has been demonstrated down through the centuries. Nehemiah declared "thou art a God ready to pardon, gracious and merciful, slow to anger, and of great kindness" (Neh 9.17). The prophet Joel appealed to the erring nation of Judah in his day: "rend your heart, and not your garments, and turn unto the Lord your God: for he is gracious and merciful, slow to anger, and of great kindness" (Joel 2.13). God's kindness has also been described as marvellous, merciful, and everlasting (Ps 31.21; 117.2; Is 54.8). Sometimes the compound word 'lovingkindness' is used, as when David confessed his sin before the Lord: "Have mercy upon me, O God, according to thy lovingkindness: according unto the multitude of thy tender mercies blot out my trangressions" (Ps 51.1).

Of all people, we should be the kindest. God has been so kind to us.

2. 8 - God's Gift

**For by grace are ye saved through faith;
and that not of yourselves: it is the gift of God:**

This and the following verse form a gospel text that many people know by heart. There must be few preachers who have not read it in public and used it to explain the way of salvation. The reason for its popularity is its simplicity and clarity.

God's grace is His unmerited favour to sinners. It stems from His heart of love and compassion for those who are lost and perishing in their sins. We are favoured to be living in a 'day of grace' when the door of salvation is still open and the message of salvation is still being proclaimed. One day, perhaps very soon, the Lord will return and the door of opportunity will be closed.

Salvation is well described in terms of the past, present and future. It involves a first step, a daily walk, and an eventual arrival at a destination. When a soul first believes in Christ, he or she has taken the step of faith. The message to the troubled jailer in Philippi was "Believe on the Lord Jesus Christ, and thou shalt be saved" (Acts 16.31). He was saved that same night. Salvation brings immediate deliverance from the penalty of sin. Continuing to live as a Christian means a daily walk in the power of the Spirit so that one is progressively sanctified. To live a holy life means to know deliverance from the power of sin. There remains a future day when, in a glorified body, the believer will arrive home in heaven and be totally free from the presence of sin.

Faith means that we accept the gift that God offers to us. God has done it all, and we believe it. He planned salvation: through the giving of His Son He provided it, and through the presentation of the gospel He offers it. We respond positively to it by faith. Faith has no merit in itself, nor is it a gift; it is the response to a gift. In normal life, when someone receives a wonderful gift, the whole focus is on the value and beauty of the gift and the kindness of the giver.

In Botswana, a child is taught to receive a gift with two hands. This is deemed to be respectful and polite. No word of thanks is necessary. The two open, empty hands say it all.

Salvation is a free gift, but it was purchased at a great price.

2.9 - No Boasting

Not of works, lest any man should boast.

One of the most difficult challenges in presenting the gospel is to help men and women see that they can do nothing to save themselves. Indeed, before God they have no merit whatsoever; in their sins, they stand guilty and condemned already. This diagnosis of the human condition runs counter to man's pride and sense of self- esteem. For this reason, many reject it, finding the gospel confrontational and objectionable. They continue to strive to work their way to heaven.

The building of the tower of Babel illustrates the efforts of men to reach heaven by their ingenuity: "Let us make brick ... let us build us a city and a tower, whose top may reach unto heaven ... let us make us a name" (Gen 11.3-4). Their efforts were in vain. God would not permit them to continue in the delusion that they did not need Him and could do it themselves.

The nation of Israel began with so much promise and the people were favoured in many ways. After hundreds of years of bondage in Egypt and forty years of wandering through the wilderness under Moses, they entered Canaan, the promised land. Under the leadership of Joshua, they conquered most of the territory and settled there. The future seemed bright, as if God's promises to Abraham were being fulfilled: God's chosen people were now in their own land under His rule. What transpired was that the people soon proved to be disobedient and rebellious, calling for a man to be their king, just like the other nations. They continued to hold on to the outer trappings of religion but their hearts were far from God.

During the life of the Lord Jesus Christ, the sect of the Pharisees displayed these negative traits, boasting of their lineage, their orthodoxy, and their superiority to others. The Lord described them as "whited sepulchres": they might initially have appeared beautiful on the outside, but within they were full of corruption and uncleanness (Mt 23.27). They feared and hated the Lord Jesus because He knew what was in their minds and hearts. Their response was to plot His death.

Today, as in all other ages, it requires much grace and wisdom on the part of those who wish to present the gospel message faithfully; it also requires the power of the Holy Spirit to enlighten the minds and convict the hearts of men.

The gospel strikes at the heart of man's pride.

2.10 - God's Masterpiece

For we are his workmanship, created in Christ Jesus unto good works, which God hath before ordained that we should walk in them.

This verse is closely linked to the two previous verses which spell out how salvation comes to us, by God's grace and through our faith. Our works have no part in it. It is all of God and we are His handiwork.

If we pause and consider the character of God, we understand that He will never create anything shoddy or second-rate. When He created this earth and all within it, He saw that everything was very good (Gen 1.31). When we become a new creation in Christ, we are not a patched up restoration; we are made anew as a veritable masterpiece with all the skill and power that God possesses (2 Cor 5.17). God sees us as being in Christ, and the beauties and glories of His Son can shine forth. We still reside in an earthly body, and we still have an old fleshly nature that can drag us down, but the reality is that we lack nothing that we require to become more and more like Christ. The challenge for us all is to cooperate fully with God and enter into the good of this knowledge.

Simply put, good works are not the means of salvation; they are the result and proof of salvation. The apostle James dealt with the matter of profession, that is a person declaring before others that they have faith. These are only words, and faith cannot be seen; however, when there are good works in evidence, then the profession is seen to be real. "What doth it profit, my brethren, though a man say he hath faith, and have not works?"; "Yea, a man may say, Thou hast faith, and I have works: shew me thy faith without thy works, and I will shew thee my faith by my works". James concluded that "faith without works is dead" (Jas 2.14, 18, 20).

All of us can rise to the occasion when there is a special need. A tragedy can provoke an emotional response and we spring into action. There is nothing wrong in this, but God wants much more from us. He wants us to continually and consistently practice good works. These works are not specified but they include all acts of kindness, big or small, to any person at any time.

Be like an expensive Swiss watch, full of good works.

2.11 - Remembering the Past

Wherefore remember, that ye being in time past Gentiles in the flesh, who are called Uncircumcision by that which is called the Circumcision in the flesh made by hands;

Another retrospective look focuses on those who were Gentiles before their conversion to Christ. They were belittled and despised by the Jews and regarded as being outside the sphere of God's blessing.

Circumcision, the cutting and removal of the male foreskin, was introduced early in the nation of Israel's history as a token of the covenant that God had made with Abraham (Gen 17.11). This ceremony involved all males and every newborn baby boy on the eighth day after birth. The nation of Israel came to pride itself in this distinctive mark and despise others who did not bear it. The Gentile nations were scornfully referred to as 'the Uncircumcision'. The Jews emphasised the outward physical sign, but so often their inward heart condition was not right before God.

In the early Church, the issue became one of grave concern as the Judaisers were insisting that this rite of circumcision was necessary for salvation.

The apostle Paul forthrightly confronted this fundamental error. In his Epistle to the Galatians, he sought to safeguard the truth of the gospel and the liberty it brought to the sinner. He pointed out that going back to law-keeping was in effect reverting to bondage. Salvation was by grace and not by merit; it was through faith but not through works. Circumcision was of no advantage whatsoever: "For in Jesus Christ neither circumcision availeth any thing, nor uncircumcision; but faith which worketh by love" (Gal 5.6). The self-righteous Jews had missed the point: "But he is a Jew, which is one inwardly; and circumcision is that of the heart, in the spirit, and not in the letter; whose praise is not of men, but of God" (Rom 2.29).

In his letter to the Colossians, Paul made a positive and spiritual application for believers based on the fact that circumcision meant the cutting off of the flesh: "In whom also ye are circumcised with the circumcision made without hands, in putting off the body of the sins of the flesh by the circumcision of Christ" (Col 2.11). The death of Christ has separated believers from sin; consequently, they should live holy lives, no longer marked by the sins of the flesh. Their new position and their condition should correspond. This was the only kind of circumcision that mattered.

The death of Christ has ended our enslavement to the flesh.

2.12 - At a Distance

That at that time ye were without Christ, being aliens from the commonwealth of Israel, and strangers from the covenants of promise, having no hope, and without God in the world:

Paul's reason for retracing their Gentile past was not to diminish them but to encourage them so that they would appreciate all the more their many blessings in Christ. Before conversion, they had been without Christ and outside the blessings that Israel enjoyed. They were idolaters, living in fear and superstition of their many false gods, but knowing little of the true and living God.

By contrast, the Jewish nation had been the recipients of God's covenant promises. Their turbulent history was the story of His unfailing goodness to a people who were often ungrateful. Sadly, few of them came to truly know Christ, and believe on Him when He was upon the earth. Ultimately, they rejected their Messiah and crucified Him. They were meant to be a channel of blessing to others, but they became proud and rebellious people who despised others. Their religion became dead, one of works and merit, instead of a vibrant and living faith in a God of grace.

Whether Gentile or Jew, personal knowledge of Christ is the essential feature of true Christianity. God can only be known through Christ who declared that "I am the way, the truth, and the life: no man cometh unto the Father, but by me" (Jn 14.6). This is an exclusive claim. The solemn reality is that without Christ sinners are lost and on a pathway to judgment and eternal separation from God. The saddest words in the verse are these – "having no hope".

In the field of healthcare, one has to convey bad news on occasions. A diagnosis may be such that medical science cannot offer a cure. I recall, early in my medical career, having to confirm this with one patient whose brother had previously died from cancer. I tried to convey the news gently, but once the patient learned that he had the same condition, he asked to be moved to a side ward, and within a few days he passed away. He was not noticeably unwell at the time, but it was clear that he lost the will to live. He had concluded that there was no hope.

To be without God and without Christ means to be without hope.

2.13 – Brought Near

But now in Christ Jesus ye who sometimes were far off are made nigh by the blood of Christ.

Another wonderful contrast extols the sacrificial work that Christ accomplished through His death upon the cross. In Christ, the Gentile believers had been brought nigh. At one time they had been far off in their sins, but now they were near in Him.

Once again the blood of Christ is mentioned. This brings to the fore Christ's sacrifice. In chapter one, His blood is the means of our redemption and forgiveness. Here His blood is the means of our inclusion in an intimate relationship with God.

In the prevailing religious climate, there seems to be a growing reluctance to say much about the blood of Christ in gospel proclamation. The doctrine of His substitutionary death and punishment on our account is regarded by some to be unjust. Others regard the truths of sacrifice and blood-shedding as being unsuited to our modern sophisticated age. Nevertheless, we must hold firmly to the Word of God, whatever the changing opinions and philosophies of men might be.

The Scriptures teach that the work Christ accomplished through His death and the shedding of His blood is the basis of our blessings:

forgiveness	Eph 1.7
redemption	1 Pet 1.18-19
justification	Rom 5.9
reconciliation	Eph 2.13
peace	Col 1.20
cleansing	Rev 1.5
sanctification	Heb 13.12

In the early Church, there were constant challenges to avoid a two-tier Christianity in which Gentile Christians would still be regarded as second class. Feelings of racial superiority on the part of converted Jews did not suddenly disappear. Good men like Peter and Barnabas were not unaffected when they were pressurised by the Judaisers. It took a Paul to see with clarity the glorious liberty that all believers should enjoy in equal measure. In this verse his words are reassuring; the truth of them would still have needed to be absorbed and assimilated into the daily lives of the believers.

So near, so very near to God, nearer I cannot be;
For in the person of His Son, I am as near as He.

C. Paget

2.14 - Our Peace

**For he is our peace, who hath made both one,
and hath broken down the middle wall of partition between us;**

Christ Himself is the peace of both Jew and Gentile. The emphasis here is not so much on what He has done but on who He is. Those who trust Him are incorporated into Him, being reconciled to God and reconciled to one another. Oneness in Him means that enmity has been replaced by peace.

While it is convenient to refer to the believers in the early Church as Gentle Christians or Jewish Christians, regarding the problems they had to overcome, it is perhaps better to keep in mind that in Christ these distinctions were done away with and each had an equal footing in Him: "There is neither Jew nor Greek [Gentile], there is neither bond nor free, there is neither male nor female: for ye are all one in Christ Jesus" (Gal 3.28).

The dividing wall of partition was a formidable obstacle indeed, more like the Berlin Wall than a thin stud wall separating two rooms in a family home. Humanly speaking, there would have been no way of overcoming it. Gentile proselytes were received into Judaism only after they had renounced their former lives and undergone circumcision, and other Gentiles known as 'God-fearers' who were attracted to the monotheism of Judaism and its moral code of behaviour but had not gone the full distance in becoming Jews (Acts 13.50; 17.4, 17; 18.7). On the whole, however, the Gentiles were regarded as being no better than unclean dogs. The sect of the Pharisees went out of their way to treat them with scorn and disdain.

In Jerusalem, the structural plan of Herod's temple illustrated the barrier of separation. The Court of the Gentiles was the outermost area beyond which the Gentiles could not proceed. Further inside and closer to the Holy Place were other areas used exclusively by the Jews. Any Gentiles found transgressing these boundaries risked the death penalty.

In Christ, all such divisions have been done away with and every child of God has equal access to the Father. It remains for us to overcome our natural prejudice concerning racial, social, and educational backgrounds, and live out what we say we believe. By God's grace this can be done.

Oneness in Christ should not only be professed but also practised.

2.15 – One New Man

Having abolished in his flesh the enmity, even the law of commandments contained in ordinances; for to make in himself of twain one new man, so making peace.

Paul's focus here is still the Jew-Gentile divide and the antagonism that had prevailed. Christ through His death had nullified the dividing influence of the Mosaic Law which in many ways had defined the Jewish nation and confirmed to them their separateness from others. In the following centuries, the Jews had added multiple man-made rules to the laws God had given; the Pharisees were outwardly meticulous about adhering to all of these requirements.

The principle that Christ introduced was no longer law but grace. Grace had brought the blessings of salvation to both Jew and Gentile and elevated them to a higher plane. The old was done away with and in its place was something completely new and greater by far. Christ's new creation is described as "one new man".

The death of Christ has accomplished so much and has brought together not only Jew and Gentile but people of all races and cultures. It is truly a wonderful experience to travel to distant places on other continents and to immediately feel a strong unifying bond of love with people who in many ways are so different. They speak a different language, wear different clothes, eat different food and have quite different customs, and yet in Christ, we find that we have so much in common.

It may well be argued that antagonistic and divisive issues remained within the early Church. The peace with God that Christ had made through the blood of His cross (Col 1.20) did not always translate into peace among His followers. That was true in those early days as the devil sought to destroy all that Christ was building and frustrate God's plan. The devil believes in 'divide and rule'. It has always been his evil design to separate men and women from God, and also one from another.

The same challenges apply today. The truth of our position in Christ is not always reflected in our spiritual condition. In other words, the practice often lags behind the theory. Human weakness means that fulfilling God's will for our lives is often a slow and sometimes painful learning process. We require constant commitment and effort to be those who are at peace with our brothers and sisters in Christ.

In a world of strife and division, Christ is still the greatest peacemaker.

2.16 - Reconciled to God

And that he might reconcile both unto God in one body by the cross, having slain the enmity thereby:

Reconciliation is one of the great gospel themes. It goes far beyond what is considered to be reconciliation in the world at large. In South Africa, following the fall of apartheid, the new government established a Truth and Reconciliation Commission. The intention was that people from both sides of the political divide should come forward to testify to the crimes they had committed. Following their full confession, some of these people were granted amnesty. It was the hope that after this long process, former enemies could come together and move forward in peace and harmony. Some were able to do so, but others were not. It had always been clear that gross injustices had been perpetrated by both sides and many innocent lives were lost. It also became evident that some still harboured resentment and felt that injustice remained.

When we come to the Bible and what it teaches of our reconciliation to God, there are marked differences. The first of these is that God has perpetrated no injustice whatsoever. He has remained as He always has been, a God of righteousness and truth. It is we sinners who have offended Him. A second important difference is that God, the offended party, has taken the initiative to bring us back to Himself. In love and mercy He has sought us who were at a distance from Himself. Thirdly, He has exacted the necessary justice on Another, His well-beloved Son. On the cross, Christ suffered and bore the judgment that was our due. This is what Paul teaches here and also affirms in other Scriptures: "God was in Christ, reconciling the world unto himself, not imputing their trespasses unto them ... For he [God] hath made him [Christ] to be sin for us, who knew no sin; that we might be made the righteousness of God in him" (2 Cor 5.19, 21).

The enmity that existed between God and us because of our sin has been removed. In the previous verse we learnt that it has been nullified. Here we learn that it has been put to death. When Christ died, the barrier of sin and the curse of the law were removed. Everything that separated sinners from God and from each other was overcome. Jew and Gentile can be brought together in one body, united in Christ and united to Him.

A holy God can never sweep sin under the carpet.

2.17 - Peace Proclaimed

And came and preached peace to you which were afar off, and to them that were nigh.

Christ was the promised Prince of Peace. Hundreds of years before He was born, Isaiah prophesied: "For unto us a child is born, unto us a son is given: and the government shall be upon his shoulder: and his name shall be called Wonderful, Counsellor, The mighty

God, The everlasting Father, The Prince of Peace. Of the increase of his government and peace there shall be no end" (Is 9.6-7). The first prediction was fulfilled at Bethlehem. The angels announced the Saviour's birth: "Glory to God in the highest, and on earth peace, good will toward men" (Lk 2.14). The full manifestation of His kingdom power and glory is yet to be revealed. This troubled and divided world will at last have a majestic Sovereign who will bring peace to every corner of the globe.

When the Lord told His disciples, "Think not that I am come to send peace on earth: I came not to send peace, but a sword" (Mt 10.34), He was explaining to them the cost of following Him and alerting them to the reality that they all must face: loyalty to Christ would produce opposition. They might find this even in their homes when family members did not share their faith and convictions. In mentioning the sword, Christ was not advocating a holy war in the manner of the Crusades. We recall that when Peter drew his sword in anger and vengeance at Christ's arrest in Gethsemane, Christ rebuked him: "Put up again thy sword into his place: for all they that take the sword shall perish with the sword" (Mt 26.52). Thereafter, Christ was brought "as a lamb to the slaughter" (Is 53.7). He went willingly and submissively to the cross.

Shortly before His crucifixion, Christ comforted the disciples with these words: "Peace I leave with you, my peace I give unto you: not as the world giveth, give I unto you. Let not your heart be troubled, neither let it be afraid" (Jn 14.27). After His resurrection, He commissioned them to go forth with the gospel. Through the preaching of the gospel worldwide, His message of peace has gone forth to Jews and Gentile alike.

Our peace does not depend on circumstances around us, but on Christ within us.

2.18 – Access Granted

For through him we both have access by one Spirit unto the Father.

The Jewish nation is its early history was always aware of God's presence in their midst. The tabernacle, a portable tent-like structure, was constructed and raised up in the wilderness. God did as He had promised and came to dwell in their midst: "And let them make me a sanctuary; that I may dwell among them" (Ex 25.8). On that notable day, a cloud covered the tent and the glory of the Lord filled it (Ex 40.34). Moses was not able to enter. The cloud signified that God's presence remained with them. It also guided them as a pillar of cloud by day and a pillar of fire by night. When the cloud moved, they moved; when it stopped, they stopped.

Access into the tabernacle was restricted. Only the priests from the tribe of Levi could enter the court and the Holy Place. Only the high priest, once a year on the Day of Atonement, could enter the Holy of the Holies, the innermost compartment where God dwelt above the mercy seat which covered the ark of the covenant. The high priest could only do so after first entering with incense and then afterwards with blood. The outstanding lesson was that God was holy, and sinful men were at a distance from Him. If that was the understanding of most Jews, even more restrictive was the position of the Gentiles. We have already considered how they were kept at a distance from the temple in Jerusalem.

Through the death of Christ, all barriers to close and intimate fellowship with God have been removed. Within the short space of this verse, we have mention of all three Persons of the Godhead: Christ, the Son; the Holy Spirit; and God, the Father. Every believer in Christ is welcome before the throne of God. This applies to any moment of any day, in any place, under any circumstances. The indwelling Holy Spirit leads us there. This is truly amazing! We do not need to go through tiers of protocol or piles of red tape to arrange an appointment. It need not be a hurried few minutes, and we need not compete with others for the Father's attention. He is there for us, all the time. We should go there often.

The door into God's presence is always open.

2.19 - Together in God's Family

**Now therefore ye are no more strangers and foreigners,
but fellowcitizens with the saints,
and of the household of God;**

The complete transformation and elevated position of Gentile believers in Christ meant that they had equal citizenship in God's kingdom and equal rights in His family. They too had been set apart for God, as the word 'saint' means. Formerly they were at a distance but now had been brought near. Paul was at pains to make these truths crystal clear as he summed them up.

He would have been fully aware that even within a closely-knit group there are hierarchies and circles within the circle. These differences can be expressed in subtle or not so subtle ways. The Jews were a pertinent example of this. They all laid claim to a common identity but within their ranks, there were factions and those who regarded themselves as a cut above the rest. The Pharisees were proud and considered themselves to be superior, so much so that they offended Christ and incurred His sternest words of condemnation.

In the world today the principle of equality is loudly trumpeted by politicians and other civic leaders. They do not mind ordinary people having equal opportunity, as long as they themselves retain their privileged position over the rest. The cynic may claim with apparent justification that 'all men are equal, but some are more equal than others'; and 'there is one law for the rich but another for the poor'. True Christianity is meant to confound these mockers and sceptics.

Conversion does not suddenly make us free from prejudice. Within the early Church tensions remained along racial lines. When problems of apparent discrimination arose, these were acknowledged and dealt with, one by one. A case in point was the matter of distribution of aid to widows (Acts 6.1-7). In Ephesians, and in other letters he wrote, Paul was laying the foundation of the essential truth that was to guide the believers as they sought to move forward and make spiritual progress in their individual lives and corporate testimony. Former Jews and former Gentiles were to sit down and break bread together as one in Christ.

All of us are learners and sometimes, to our shame, we learn so slowly. Grace has been the operating principle in the matter of our salvation. It should continue to govern how we think of our brothers and sisters in Christ who have also come into the blessings of that same grace.

Happy is the man who has learnt to love all of God's children and afford each the utmost respect.

2.20 - The sure Foundation

And are built upon the foundation of the apostles and prophets, Jesus Christ himself being the chief corner stone;

Paul now introduces the metaphor of a building, actually a temple, to explain that all believers have a firm foundation in Christ. The apostles and prophets assisted in laying that foundation by proclaiming Jesus Christ as Saviour and Lord. This is akin to the Lord's words to Peter after he confessed that Jesus was the Christ: "Thou art Peter, and upon this rock I will build my church; and the gates of hell shall not prevail against it" (Mt 16.18). The rock was not Peter, but Christ Himself whom Peter had just extolled. Even after Pentecost, the transformed and energised apostle had his moments of wavering and instability.

The apostles were those men chosen by Christ and personally commissioned by Him to take His life-giving message far and near. The prophets mentioned here were those men in the early Church (not the Old Testament prophets) who employed their gift of prophecy and transmitted fresh but partial revelations from God. Both of these roles fell away with the completion of the Scriptures, the full revelation of God's will to mankind.

The word order, "Jesus Christ", emphasises the man who lived down here who is now in heaven as the exalted Christ. He alone is the 'foundation' and 'chief corner stone'. The mixed metaphors show that not only is Christ the foundation, providing all the underlying strength and stability that a building needs, but also He is that keystone from which all other measurements are taken. When a builder marks out a building construction, he requires a constant reference point. Today it might be a short metal stake, a datum peg, but this must never be moved, and should always be referred to. In this sense, we understand Christ is everything to the Church: the architect, the builder, the foundation itself, and the constant point of reference.

We cannot forget that He was once the rejected stone: "Jesus saith unto them, Did ye never read in the scriptures, The stone which the builders rejected, the same is become the head of the corner?" We agree wholeheartedly with the Psalmist's conclusion: "This is the Lord's doing; it is marvellous in our eyes" (Mt 21.42 ; Ps 118.23).

> *On Christ, the solid rock, I stand;*
> *All other ground is sinking sand.*
> Edward Mote

2.21 - Framed Together

**In whom all the building fitly framed together
groweth unto an holy temple in the Lord:**

The foundation has been laid already; there will never need to be another foundation. Christ is continuing with the ongoing work of adding the superstructure. The bricks, or "[living] stones" as Peter describes them (1 Pet 2.5), are individual believers. Christ as the Master Builder, prepares each of them and then fits them perfectly into the most appropriate place in the building. Each stone is supported and strengthened by the others.

Standing before the Western Wall in Jerusalem, one observes that the huge blocks of limestone, known as ashlars, were not mortared together. These date from the time of Herod who added a surrounding enclosure to the temple. They were so expertly cut and dressed, that they could be put in position dry. Originally, in the construction of the first temple erected by Solomon, the command went forth that there was to be "neither hammer nor axe nor any tool of iron heard in the house, while it was in building" (1 Kings 6.7). This preparatory work was performed off-site.

Modern buildings are designed to withstand all sorts of stresses and strains from both natural disasters such as earthquakes and flooding, and accidental or intentional manmade catastrophes such as explosions or arson. However, should there have been defective planning, shoddy workmanship or the use of inferior materials, cracks and other defects can appear. Such buildings are often declared to be unsafe and therefore they are condemned.

These illustrate the two main ways in which the devil has sought to destroy what Christ is building. The Church has been opposed from without and weakened from within. It is difficult for us to see the whole picture when there are so many cracks and divisions, even among Christians today. God sees the complete picture and a perfect whole. We must take encouragement from Christ's words that reassure us His building will prevail. The Church is still standing and still growing. It has an unshakeable foundation.

"Holiness becometh thine house, O Lord, for ever" was what the Psalmist wrote (Ps 93.5). God's house is made up of each of us and we either adorn it or we mar it by the way we live.

Be a builder and binder in God's house, not a destroyer or a divider; be one who beautifies it, not one who defiles it.

2.22 - Built Together

In whom ye also are builded together for an habitation of God through the Spirit.

The Gentile saints were being reminded of their privileged position in Christ as part of the building where God was pleased to dwell. In the tabernacle and Solomon's temple, His dwelling place was the inner sanctuary, the Holy of Holies. Today the Holy Spirit of God permanently resides within every believer. This means that in the individual sense, in the local assembly, as well as in the corporate sense, God dwells in us.

Many of the Ephesian Christians had once been idolaters. They were closely associated with the temple to Diana, considered to be one of the seven wonders of the ancient world. It was twice the size of any other known temple in those days and was said to have had originally 127 massive marble columns arranged in double rows. The visual impact of such a vast and magnificent building was considerable; it would have dominated the minds and hearts of the people before conversion. However, Paul was now filling their eyes with a spiritual vision far more impressive than anything of earth. Samuel Medley (1738-1799) captured something of the wonder of it:

> *View the vast building, see it rise:*
> *The work how great! the plan how wise!*
> *O wondrous fabric! pow'r unknown*
> *That rests it on the "Living Stone".*

Once again the word 'together' is employed to stress the essential unity of God's people in God's building. Unity is a theme that runs right through the Scriptures and for good reason. It produces strength, support, stability, and blessing. Psalm 133 reminds us of this: "How good and how pleasant it is for brethren to dwell together in unity! ... for there the Lord commanded the blessing, even life for evermore" (Ps 133.1, 3).

Disunity produces strife, weakness, and division. It may be caused by pride or jealousy. At other times it is a result of serious disagreements concerning doctrine and practice. The outcome of division is defeat and tragedy.

The verse indicates that God's construction is ongoing and that He is performing it according to His plan. We too have our part to play in fellowship with God. Paul exhorted the Corinthians to make sure they were adding that which was of true value: "But let every man take heed how he buildeth thereupon" (1 Cor 3.10).

God has put us together and expects us to keep together.

Chapter 3

Richness in Christ

The mysteries revealed are that the Gentiles are fellow-heirs in the Church which is Christ's body, and that the Church will witness eternally to God's wisdom.
Paul's ministry was to preach the riches of Christ.
Paul's second prayer was that the saints should be strong, stable, and loving.

3.1 - Paul the Prisoner

**For this cause I Paul, the prisoner of
Jesus Christ for you Gentiles,**

The personal reference at this point in the letter provides a break. The cause to which Paul referred is more likely to be the matters he had already addressed rather than the new subject he was about to introduce, the mystery of Christ. The following section, vv. 2-13, is another long clause in Greek, after which Paul repeats the phrase, "for this cause" in v. 14. Paul tended to 'go off on a tangent' as we might say, but under the inspiration of the Spirit of God, his thought-flow was controlled and purposeful at all times. He was not rambling in the way we might do when we lose track of what we are saying or where we mean to go in a conversation.

He never referred to himself as 'a prisoner of Caesar', even though he was being held by the imperial authorities in Rome. He saw his circumstances as having come about because of his loyalty to Christ in proclaiming the gospel wherever he went. It was all in God's plan for his life. Furthermore, if his Lord was in control, he did not need to worry or fret. If Christ opened the door for his release, no authority on earth would be able to close it.

It has been well remarked that all of us are prisoners to something. Some are captivated by sinful pleasure. Others lust for wealth, power and position and these things control their every thought, word and action. Men are never so free as they claim to be. The apostle Paul was committed to Christ and regarded himself as the willing bondslave to his Master. Christ was his life and his goal: "For to me to live is Christ, and to die is gain"; "that I may win Christ ..." (Phil 1.21; 3.8). Paul viewed himself as having no rights outside of the right to follow Christ; he had no interests outside of his devotion to fulfil his Master's will and please Him in all things.

Paul never complained about his prison conditions: the poor food, lack of hygiene, an uncomfortable bed or cruel guards. Despite being confined, the prison could not keep him from praying or praising, from preaching the gospel or penning such wonderful letters. His mind soared freely heavenwards, and in any case, the Lord was by his side.

After conversion, Paul was captivated by Jesus Christ
for the rest of his life.

3.2 - Paul the Steward

If ye have heard of the dispensation of the grace of God
which is given me to you-ward:

Paul was not doubting whether or not the Ephesians had heard of his special commission from the Lord. He was simply reminding them that since they already knew, they would understand the implications of it. The apostle regarded this commission as a sacred trust or stewardship. Like all of God's purposes, it was marked by grace from start to finish.

Firstly, God planned to bless underserving sinners, both Jew and Gentile. This was grace indeed. Secondly, God saved a fanatical, self-righteous Jew known for his fierce persecution of Christians. He was the one chosen to be the apostle to the Gentiles, preaching the gospel to them and also teaching them of the great blessings they shared in Christ. Paul never lost the sense of wonder at divine grace in operation in his own life. He recalled how he had once been "a blasphemer, and a persecutor, and injurious" and yet "the grace of our Lord was exceeding abundant" (1 Tim 1.13-14). The one who counted himself the chief of sinners could testify later that "by the grace of God I am what I am: and his grace which was bestowed upon me was not in vain" (1 Cor 15.10).

The idea of stewardship (here translated 'dispensation') involves faithfully preserving and passing on exactly what has been entrusted to one's care. Paul's life was a shining example of this. Even in the face of opposition and harassment, he never deviated from the truth the Lord had revealed to him. He proclaimed it, defended it, suffered for it, and he would eventually die for it.

Initially, after his conversion, he had to overcome the suspicion of the Christians who had known him only as a persecutor. He also incurred the wrath of his former Jewish countrymen who would have viewed him as a traitor to their cause. They would go on to hound him incessantly wherever he went. Surely it was only by the grace of God that he kept his sense of balance. He retained a deep love for his fellow Jews, longing for their salvation (Rom 10.1), but he also poured out his life for the Gentiles all over the Roman world, from east to west, becoming all things to all men, that he might "by all means save some" (1 Cor 9.22).

We who have received God's grace are to be channels of grace to others.

3.3 - The Revelation

How that by revelation he made known unto me the mystery; (as I wrote afore in few words,

God is a God of revelation. This means that He communicates with mankind and informs His creatures of His will and His ways. He reveals Himself, as well as revealing His purposes, so that we might get to know Him rather than just know facts about Him.

After Paul's conversion, there was a period of perhaps several years, when he had a 'desert experience' in a remote area he called Arabia (Gal 1.17). In his letter to the Galatians, Paul detailed his movements to prove that the gospel he preached was revealed to him by the Lord Himself, in isolation from other apostles in Jerusalem or elsewhere. His message was not a mishmash gathered together from various sources. At the same time, Paul was not claiming that his gospel was different from that of the other apostles, but simply that he had received it directly from the Lord. Included in the revelations he received were new teachings that he proclaimed to others: these included the 'mystery doctrines' we read of in Ephesians. Paul had already mentioned "the mystery of his [God's] will" (Eph 1.9) and he was now about to expand upon it further.

God has often prepared his servants in desert areas, where they were alone with Him. Moses received the vision of the burning bush at Horeb and heard the voice of God (Ex 3.1-4). Elijah learned lessons of dependence at the brook called Cherith, as God miraculously provided for his daily needs during a time of drought (1 Kings 17.1-7). Others like John the Baptist and even our Lord Himself spent time alone in barren, inhospitable places where they were tried and tested. As for ourselves, there are lessons that we can only learn when we are alone with God, with no noise or other distractions. We may not have to retire to a desert but we all need a quiet time in a quiet place. We read His Word and pray so that He speaks to us and we speak to Him. The inspired Scriptures are complete and contain all we need to know. It only requires us to read and dig deeper to uncover the treasure and find Him therein.

God is a God who communicates with us.
Did you hear His voice today?

3.4 - The Mystery

Whereby, when ye read, ye may understand my knowledge in the mystery of Christ)

There is some discussion among Bible students as to whether the letter to the Ephesians was intended for one specific local church or meant to be read among a group of churches in one particular area. Both this letter and the letter to the Colossians were carried by Tychicus from Rome to the province of Asia Minor (Eph 6.21; Col 4.7). We can safely say, however, that if the truth contained in these letters was good for one specific local church, then the truth was good for them all, just as it is good and vital for every believer and every local assembly today.

A handwritten copy to the Ephesians was probably read out publicly to the Christians as they assembled together. There were no fast duplicating services in those days and so when Paul speaks of reading, he means that it was read to them. One would imagine that such a letter would need to be read on several occasions if the believers were to grasp the essential doctrines and exhortations contained therein. It is unlikely that the copy was left lying around for anyone to casually pick up. It would have been carefully handled and stored.

There are no original letters ('autographs') remaining from the New Testament writings. They were written on papyrus made from compressed reeds, or vellum made from the skin of an animal. Such materials perished over time. However, there are thousands of ancient copies in existence that assist Bible scholars to examine the text of Scripture. One of the earliest, the John Rylands Fragment, is a small piece of papyrus containing five verses from John's gospel. It is thought to date from the early part of the second century. Such historical evidence is priceless.

Paul anticipated that the reading of his letter would enable the believers to understand the truth that had been revealed to him and which he was now imparting to them. There are challenges in every age and today there would seem to be a marked change in reading habits. Whatever we do, may we not neglect our Bibles but truly treasure them, reading them daily and often. It helps to keep our Bibles open, prominent and instantly accessible in our homes.

Paul to Timothy: "Give attendance to reading." (1 Tim 4.13)

3.5 - Now Revealed

**Which in other ages was not made known unto the sons of men,
as it is now revealed unto his holy apostles and prophets
by the Spirit;**

Paul had a deep knowledge of the Old Testament Scriptures, having been highly trained in the Jewish religion. He had been "brought up ... at the feet of Gamaliel, and taught according to the perfect manner of the law of the fathers" (Acts 22.3) as "a Pharisee, the son of a Pharisee" (Acts 23.6). After his conversion, he would have begun to understand that many prophecies in the Hebrew scriptures had found their fulfilment in Christ. He would also have noted as never before that God always had a plan to bless other nations as well as the Jews. But what Paul is confirming here is that the Old Testament did not reveal any doctrine concerning the Church, and how it would be formed of both Jew and Gentile standing together on the same ground. This was a fresh revelation from the Lord and entirely appropriate for a new age of grace. It was Paul's special responsibility to make this known.

In the religious world, there is a great deal of confusion about the respective places of Israel and the Church in the plan of God. Some believe that the Church under a new covenant has replaced Israel under an old covenant. By this reckoning, there is no real distinctive future for the Jewish nation. It is claimed that all of the kingdom blessings originally promised to that nation are now to be realised in the Church. The theory is that the covenants with Abraham and his descendants concerning a nation, a land, a city and a throne have all been done away with, in a literal sense.

Confusion will be avoided if we understand that God has set Israel aside for now (Rom 11.8, 15, 17, 25). The Lord is building His Church in this age. But when He returns to the air (for His Church) to call it home to heaven, Israel will again take centre stage upon the earth. The prophetic clock, as it were, will start ticking again. Divine judgment will be poured upon this earth before the Lord returns (with His Church) and sets up His millennial kingdom. Then, and only then, will all of the promises to Abraham be fulfilled in the Messiah. God's earthly nation will inherit the land and all that was promised to them. Once again a King shall reign in Zion!

Both Israel and the Church have a wonderful future.

3. 6 - The same Body

That the Gentiles should be fellowheirs, and of the same body, and partakers of his promise in Christ by the gospel:

Further details were given of the blessings that God was showering upon the Gentiles. They had become equal heirs to the divine inheritance that God has for the Church. We recall the story of Ruth in which the near kinsman to Naomi declined to take the Gentile Moabitess to be his wife because he did not want to spoil his own inheritance. Any children born to Ruth would have retained the name of her first husband and yet have equal claim to the joint inheritance. This was all too much for the near kinsman and he transferred this right to Boaz who was more than willing to meet every requirement of the law. Boaz is a picture of Christ, our Kinsman-Redeemer, who willingly paid all that was required to make us His own.

Paul used three similar words in this verse (two of them unique to Ephesians) to explain the new position of Gentiles as fellow-heirs in God's family, fellow-members in Christ's body, and fellow-partakers in the divine promises. They formerly had no part in God's promises (Eph 2.12). The force of these words means much more than saying that Gentiles had joined Jews in receiving these blessings. They mean that the two groups were so united as to become indistinguishable in Christ.

The Gentiles had once felt the stigma of exclusion from privilege, as least as far as the Jews were concerned; the Jews had once felt pride in their apparent superiority over Gentile races. Both had to make radical adjustments to their way of thinking. It was to take some time for the

Church to appreciate and practise the new order. Christianity was not to be regarded as an updated version of Judaism. Jewish believers had to remember that they had been just as sinful and needy of salvation as the Gentiles. Gentile believers had to keep before them the tremendous blessings that had been imparted to them as those who had once been steeped in idolatry and far from God. Both would require humility and love to move forward, not as two allied groups, but as one in Christ.

The Church of Christ is the greatest fellowship this world will ever see.

3. 7 - Grace and Power

Wherefore I was made a minister, according to the gift of grace of God given unto me by the effectual working of his power.

Here again, Paul expressed his sense of wonder that God would use him, in many ways such an unlikely choice, to reveal these truths. A man who was once motivated by racial pride and hateful prejudice had been shown divine grace. A divider had become a uniter. God's grace to sinners is always undeserved, equally after conversion as before it. It is a gift, not an entitlement or a reward. It has been well described as giving 'everything for nothing to those who don't deserve anything'. Paul acknowledged that to be a steward of this mystery concerning the Church required not only grace but also divine power. He was thus enabled to do what God wanted him to do. He could neither claim any self-righteousness nor any personal ability to fulfil God's purpose.

Furthermore, Paul recognised that he was divinely appointed to this specific work; he was not self-appointed. He had no say in the matter other than to ask at the beginning of his life as a Christian the all-important question: "Lord, what wilt thou have me to do?" (Acts 9.6). Paul did not baulk when it was soon revealed to him that the pathway ahead would involve great suffering and hardship. The Lord directed a man called Ananias to inform the new convert: "Go thy way: for he is a chosen vessel unto me, to bear my name before the Gentiles, and kings, and the children of Israel: For I will shew him how great things he must suffer for my name's sake" (Acts 9.15-16).

It is God's power alone that enables us to fulfil His will. His power also changes us and goes on changing us so that we become more like His own blessed Son. We need to remind ourselves that as God's children we are in daily contact with the Omnipotent. His strength is made perfect in our weakness (2 Cor 12.9). Paul confessed, "I can do all things through Christ which strengtheneth me" (Phil 4.13). We might also add that God does not employ His power wastefully or ineffectively. All that He wishes to accomplish will be fulfilled.

God will enable you to do what He wants you to do for His glory.

3. 8 - *Less than the Least*

**Unto me, who am less than the least of all saints,
is this grace given, that I should preach among the Gentiles
the unsearchable riches of Christ;**

Humility does not come easily to most people. Seeds of pride linger in all our hearts. Even when we try to act humbly, we can end up thinking too much about ourselves and how others might assess us. Those who are truly humble before God think little about themselves and care even less about the opinions of others. George Müller (1805-1895) is worth quoting: 'There was a day when I died, died to George Müller, his opinions, preferences, tastes and will; died to the world, its approval or censure; died to the approval or blame of my brethren or friends; and since then I have studied only to show myself approved unto God.'

Paul did not traffic in exaggeration. Every Bible word he wrote was couched in sincerity. It was not a show of mock humility when he described himself as being "less than the least of all saints". That is how he thought of himself. His past cruelty against innocent Christians was certainly one factor in this lowly self-assessment, causing him to write "I am the least of the apostles, that am not meet to be called an apostle, because I persecuted the church of God" (1 Cor 15.9). As mentioned before, he also regarded himself as the chief of sinners (1 Tim 1.15).

On other occasions, he related what would have been his social and religious credentials in the eyes of the world. This was not done to boast but rather to defend his ministry against those who were attacking it. He explained, "But what things were gain to me, those I counted loss for Christ" (Phil 3.7); and "God forbid that I should glory, save in the cross of our Lord Jesus Christ, by whom the world is crucified unto me, and I unto the world" (Gal 6.14).

He exulted in the gospel message concerning Christ crucified. He faithfully proclaimed it all over the Roman empire and was bold in witnessing to all he met. He knew that it was the best news that men could ever hear. It promised superabundant spiritual blessings – unfathomable and unscalable – both now, and for all eternity.

The way up in Christ's service is always the way down.

3.9 - That All May See

And to make all men see what is the fellowship of the mystery, which from the world hath been hid in God, who created all things by Jesus Christ:

Here we have the breadth of Paul's aspiration: he wanted all to hear the good news of the gospel and to experience its life-transforming power. It revealed God's love, grace, and wisdom to all mankind. He wanted to dispel the darkness in men's hearts so that all would see the wonders of what had been conceived in the heart of God.

This enlightenment would reveal the many brilliant colours in God's 'landscape', and cause men and women to appreciate the truth as well as appropriating it into their daily living. It was not merely an intellectual understanding that was needed; Paul's aim was that the believers should be spiritually strengthened by the truth and transformed by it.

The mystery referred to here is the same as the one we have considered a few verses earlier, namely that Jews and Gentiles are regarded as one and as equals in the Church. Paul's desire was only a reflection of God's plan and purpose that had been formed long before the world was made, but was now being made known through the apostle. He felt keenly his responsibility and privilege in this regard. God was the omnipotent Creator of all things. When He made the universe, He spoke and it was done. His creation was something that all men could see, revealing to them His eternal power and Godhead (Rom 1.20). While this display of His greatness had always been on display, His plan for Jew and Gentile was only recently revealed.

Perhaps we limit ourselves at times when we preach the gospel. We rightly emphasise the urgent personal need of sinners. We might speak of their sinful past and also explain the glorious eternal future that is promised in Christ. It would seem that Paul had a much wider perspective and would have incorporated the universal aspects of divine purpose. While the Jew-Gentile divide might seem to be only history to us now, the implications of their unity in the body of Christ are just as relevant and necessary today. Racial tensions can spoil the oneness that God is looking for among His people. The devil well knows this and keeps busy trying to stir up these divisive attitudes.

God enlightens our darkness through His revealed Word.

3.10 - God's Wisdom made Known

**To the intent that now unto the principalities and powers
in heavenly places might be known by the church
the manifold wisdom of God,**

God has in view that His wisdom will be seen in the Church and made known by it. To the sceptical onlooker the Church today must seem like a divided conglomeration of opposing factions. The multiplicity of denominations and the obvious disparities in doctrine only add to the general confusion. News headlines exposing moral and financial scandals in the religious world fuel cynicism and the rejection of anything connected with religion.

The eye of God, however, sees what we could never see: He sees the true among the false, the wheat among the chaff, and the gold among the dross. In a day to come all that is not genuine will be swept away, leaving that which is beautiful and pure to show forth the multicoloured glories of God's design. People from all over the world, both Jew and Gentile, will be seen to be complete in Christ. Despite differences of race and culture, social and economic status, the Church will be seen to be truly one, a complete and glorious body under the headship of Christ.

The heavenly powers above, angels and demons alike, will gaze upon the Church and realise the magnificence of the divine plan. As we have learned, that plan was conceived in eternity past before the worlds were made. It is being fulfilled in time as Christ continues to build His Church so that even now angels wonder at it. It will be on display for all eternity to come as a testimony to the wisdom of God.

In the Gospel of Matthew (Mt 13.1-52) the Lord Jesus Christ told a series of parables concerning His kingdom and its development. Most of them referred to agricultural elements such as seed, soil, and weeds. Another referred to a harvest of fish from the sea. Two other parables, however, seem to stand out on their own: one concerned treasure hidden in a field; the other referred to something singularly beautiful – a pearl of great price. Bible students consider this to be a picture of the Church and the price that Christ was prepared to pay, selling "all that he had", to make it His own. The beauty of the pearl is a reflection of the glorious wisdom of God that will one day be put on full display.

God's wisdom outshines all the other wisdom of men.

3.11 - God's Purpose in Christ

According to the eternal purpose which he purposed in Christ Jesus our Lord:

God's purposes for the ages are wrapped up in His Son, the Lord Jesus Christ. They were formed and framed in Him, and will be fulfilled in Him. And all of our blessings depend on Him as well.

Christ is the eternal Son of God. He knew the love of the Father and reciprocated that love from before the creation. Before He went to the cross He prayed to the Father, "Father ... thou lovedst me before the foundation of the world" (Jn 17.24).

Christ is the eternal Word. John the apostle tells us that "In the beginning was the Word, and the Word was with God, and the Word was God." (Jn 1.1). Christ is not only the Creator of all things, but He is also the revealer of the Father. God has spoken to us in His Son (Heb 1.1-2), and Christ's words shall never pass away (Lk 21.33).

Christ's work is eternal. God's plan of salvation was not conceived as an emergency. Christ was foreknown before the foundation of the world to be the sacrificial Lamb who would be slain (1 Pet 1.19-20). When we believe in Him we receive eternal salvation, and when we get to heaven, the Lamb will be the theme of our perpetual praise (Rev 5.13).

Christ's priesthood is eternal. The nation of Israel knew only a succession of high priests, one replacing another after death. Christ is now in heaven as our Great High Priest; "Thou art a priest for ever after the order of Melchisedec" (Heb 5.6). He is the unchanging Christ in whom we can trust implicitly, "the same yesterday, and to day, and for ever" (Heb 13.8).

Christ's kingship is eternal. Today He sits upon the throne where He receives glory and honour and praise (Rev 4.9-10) as the One "that liveth for ever and ever". Here upon earth He is still the rejected King, but when He returns and sets up His millennial kingdom, every knee shall bow, and every tongue shall confess that Jesus Christ is Lord, to the glory of God the Father (Phil 2.10-11). The kingdom of this world will become "the kingdom of our Lord, and of his Christ; and he shall reign for ever and ever" (Rev 11.15 RV).

God's blessings in Christ have no end.

3.12 - Our Access to Him

**In whom we have boldness and access with confidence
by the faith of him.**

There is a remarkable transition, turning from the vast creation, the principalities and powers in heavenly places, and the eternal purpose of God, to focus upon us as individuals, small and insignificant as we might appear. Paul included himself in this verse which speaks of a believer's access directly into the presence of God. This privilege is intensely personal and intimate. Christ has made it possible: through faith in Him we can come unto the Father (Jn 14.6).

The Israelite was well aware of the barriers between himself and God. When conscious of sin, he could only come to the gate of the tabernacle and no further. Even when he came expressly to worship, the same applied. He stood at the gate. It was only the priests who could minister in the court of the tabernacle or the Holy Place. Furthermore, all Israel knew that it was only the high priest on one day of the year who could venture into the Holy of Holies where God dwelt. The Gentile believers came from a completely different background, but they too had come to realise the holiness of God and their sinfulness before Him. Through the death of Christ, all barriers to personal fellowship with God had been removed.

The boldness spoken of is not brashness or careless bravado. It is a holy confidence and fixed assurance that all barriers have been removed. We have no reason to fear and run away as Adam did, but rather we have every reason to draw near. We have the liberty to speak freely and fully to the Father, unburdening our hearts (Heb 4.16; 10.19).

In this age of mobile phones, most of us know the frustration of failing to make a call for one reason or another: we have no credit, the contact is unavailable or engaged, we are out of range, or the network is down. No such problems need hinder us from speaking to our God at any time, in any place, or under any circumstances. We are warmly welcomed and He gives us His full attention. He will not mind if we are too wordy or cannot find the right words at all; He will not protest if we are repetitious or persistent. Should we spend the whole day speaking with Him, He will not complain; in fact, He encourages it!

We are always welcome in God's presence.

3.13 – Tribulations

Wherefore I desire that ye faint not at my tribulations for you, which is your glory.

Paul was concerned that the reports of his imprisonment and the opposition he had experienced might stumble the believers and cause them to be discouraged. He was prepared to face the difficulties and pay the price that was involved in fulfilling God's purpose for his life:

taking the gospel to the Gentiles involved hardship and suffering for him, but the outcome was much blessing to others. It was well worth it, as far as Paul was concerned. He hoped that they would see this positive outcome and not focus on the negatives.

When writing to the Christians at Philippi, Paul had noted that the effect of his imprisonment produced blessing even within the ranks of the Roman authorities. His clear, bold testimony was such that some officials had been saved in Caesar's household: "my bonds in Christ are manifest in all the palace, and in all other places" (Phil 1.13; 4.22). Furthermore, others had been emboldened by his example to proclaim the gospel more zealously in their own areas. Perversely, some of his enemies hoped that if they also promoted the gospel, the result would be increased suffering for the apostle, "supposing to add affliction to my bonds" (Phil 1.16). Rather than producing an outburst of righteous indignation, Paul confessed that whatever the motive, true or false, he was able to rejoice that the gospel was being preached!

Paul's prison letter to Philemon speaks of a slave who absconded and ran away to Rome. The implication was that he had robbed his master and hoped he might escape judgment by hiding himself among the vast population of Rome. It was a cosmopolitan melting pot with slaves from all parts of the empire mingling there. Onesimus, the slave, came into contact with Paul, the prisoner, and was converted.

One can imagine what might have been the frustrations for Paul, a man who loved to travel everywhere with the gospel, of being confined and under house arrest. As we have seen already, he was as busy for His Lord inside the prison as outside of it. Paul had hoped to testify to Christ in Rome (Rom 1.15), but he probably never thought that he would do so from prison. It was all in the plan of God.

Being a blessing to others may come at a price.

3.14 - Bowed Knees

For this cause I bow my knees unto the Father of our Lord Jesus Christ,

Perhaps it was both a combination of considering such great truths as well as having a concern for the spiritual welfare of the saints that caused the apostle to bow in prayer. (the prayer had begun at the first verse of the chapter, "for this cause", and is taken up again here). There is often a good deal of discussion about how we should pray to God: the posture employed, the forms of address, and the language used. The Bible does guide us with some of these issues, presenting us with a great variety of different prayers offered in different circumstances. It would be unwise to codify all of these into a list of man-made rules. A friend of mine, now in heaven, had a personal conviction that we should stand to praise and bow to plead. Certainly, bowed knees do convey an attitude of mind and heart that is humble, submissive and reverent before Almighty God.

The access every Christian has into God's presence means that both formal public and more informal private prayers are acceptable to Him. What God does expect though on every occasion is sincerity in our approach to Him. The Lord castigated the Pharisees for their love of showy and longwinded prayers in prominent public places; they hoped that others would be suitably impressed (Mt 6.5).

Some of the most sincere prayers have been the shortest and were offered in situations where bowing was not an option. When Peter was sinking in the sea he cried out, "Lord, save me!". His brief emergency prayer was heard and immediately answered (Mt 14.30-31). King Hezekiah was lying in bed, terminally ill, when he turned his face to the wall and prayed. The Lord heard him and extended his life for a further fifteen years (2 Kgs 20.1-7). King David's psalms were prayers offered in a wide variety of circumstances and often he mingled praise with fervent intercession. Many other examples are found in the Scriptures of men and women who believed in prayer and reached out in their need to a God who heard.

There is the act of prayer but there is also the atmosphere and attitude of prayer. We can go through the day, frequently lifting our voices to God. When we cannot find the right words, even our sighs, groans, and tears are interpreted by the Spirit of God and are heard in the throne-room of heaven (Rom 8.26-27).

Whether or not you can bow your knees, always bow your heart before God.

3.15 - The Family

Of whom the whole family in heaven and earth is named,

The Fatherhood of God in the previous verse presents to us a picture that we can relate to from our own experience of family life, especially those of us who have known the care and counsel of our fathers. This is not the case with everyone in the world today: some people have never known their fathers and others have been scarred by fathers who were neglectful or abusive. Sadly, broken and dysfunctional families are all too common.

How big is the family, or fatherhood, mentioned here? In the context, does it relate to the whole natural creation of God, or is it referring only to those of the Church who comprise His spiritual family? All who have been born into this world are part of God's creation; whereas only those who have been born again through faith in Christ can claim to be His believing children (Jn 1.12). Believers have the privilege of intimacy in approaching God and addressing Him as "Abba, Father" (Rom 8.15; Gal 4.6). Perhaps the wider thought applies here but it does not negate the more specific focus.

Fatherhood originated with God and takes its name from His character. He is a God of love and care. This was seen at the beginning of creation when He provided all that Adam and Eve required. Everything that He made was good and for their blessing. He is also a God of truth and righteousness, setting boundaries for our first parents and warning them of the consequences of disobedience. By doing this God wanted to protect them, but they chose to act independently and sinned against Him. This resulted in judgment.

Earthly fatherhood should reflect these aspects of God's character - His love, care, protection, and righteousness. His children have never lacked anything that they needed; they have never been overcome by their enemies when they trusted in Him. The God who was patient and longsuffering with the erring nation of Israel has been patient with us too when we have stumbled on the pathway. He is truly "the Father of mercies, and the God of all comfort" (2 Cor 1.3).

Our heavenly Father remains the greatest example for all earthly fathers.

3.16 - Spiritual Strength

That he would grant you, according to the riches of his glory, to be strengthened with might by his Spirit in the inner man;

Paul in his second prayer has no doubts concerning God's desire to enable His children to live for Him. He knows that there are divine resources available for every Christian, to meet every need and provide for every situation. The riches of His glory are linked to "the riches of his grace" (Eph 1.7); they cannot be merited or measured. God's supplies are incalculable and inexhaustible. The phrase, "according to", means that His abundant giving is in proportion to His vast supplies. God is not stingy and He is never impoverished by giving – there is always more.

His love has no limits, His grace has no measure,
His power no boundary known unto men;
For out of His infinite riches in Jesus
He giveth, and giveth, and giveth again.

Annie J. Flint

It is always a good thing to feel our weakness before Him and our complete dependence upon Him. By this we avoid any self-confidence or any thought that we can cope by relying upon our own strength or ingenuity. God is not just there for emergencies; He is there for every moment of every day. We need Him every hour.

The indwelling Holy Spirit of God is the One who enables us to live for God and enjoy all the blessings that He has for us. The Spirit works within us, moulding our spiritual nature and character so that we have the strength to go on. He is the power that we need. However, He does require our cooperation because sometimes we may ignore His guidance and choose our own contrary way. When we do this, we nurture the old nature, starve the new nature, and personally grieve the divine Holy Spirit within us (Eph 4.30).

Paul had just been speaking of his suffering for Christ. How had he been able to endure it and see beyond it? Surely he was only able to do so by divine power. Similarly for us, the power that saved us is the same power that can sustain us, sanctify us, and strengthen us to face the ups and downs of life on the journey home to heaven.

God's strength is made perfect in our weakness.

3.17 – Spiritual Stability

**That Christ may dwell in your hearts
by faith; that ye, being rooted and grounded in love,**

It would be a mistake to regard Paul's requests as a random selection of blessings he desired for his believing friends in Ephesus. His requests were all interdependent. His first prayer had focused more on the need to understand their blessings in Christ; this second prayer goes beyond that to their need of experiencing the same – from revelation to realisation, or from theory to practice.

He desired that Christ would not only abide but also be at home in their hearts through His Spirit. The idea of the strengthening Holy Spirit is synonymous with the indwelling Christ. This was not a process in which one prepared the way for another. At the moment of conversion, the Holy Spirit indwells and seals the new believer (Eph 1.13). According to Scripture, it is equally true that the Father and the Son take up residence within the child of God, just as Christ explained: "If a man love me, he will keep my words: and my Father will love him, and we will come unto him, and make our abode with him" (Jn 14.23). These combined truths are beyond our full comprehension, but they can be believed and enjoyed. Perhaps the main thrust of the truth in this verse is that Christ should be central to the believer's affections and also be in full control.

Faith and love cannot be easily separated. One promotes the other so that the two grow together as an unbreakable bond. Paul indicated that the operation of these graces would give stability to the believers. Just as a tree with a deep root system can withstand the storm, so too can the child of God who is growing in faith and love. Just as a building with a solid foundation will not be shaken apart by the earthquake, so too will be the one who trusts in the Lord and who knows that "all things work together for good to them that love God" (Rom 8.28). The apostle James turned to a picture of the sea to portray the instability of one whose faith wavers: "He that wavereth is like a wave of the sea driven with the wind and tossed ... A double minded man is unstable in all his ways" (Jas 1.6-8).

May we stand firm and true for Christ today.

3.18 – Spiritual Understanding

May be able to comprehend with all saints what is the breadth, and length, and depth, and height;

Once again Paul's love and desire for all of God's people stand as a challenge to some of us who are at times narrow and limited in our affections. We find it difficult to have a heart for other Christians, particularly if they do not agree with our doctrine and practices. The sad result of this is that our pride corrupts us and hinders our growth in becoming more like Christ.

Paul never overlooked the vital necessity of soundness in doctrine and godly order in practice. He rebuked the Corinthians for their failings in these respects, and yet his love for them was clear and unashamed: "For out of much affliction and anguish of heart I wrote unto you with many tears; not that ye should be grieved, but that ye might know the love which I have more abundantly unto you" (2 Cor 2.4). He had a burden of care for "all the churches", the good and the bad, those that were easy to love and those that were much less so (2 Cor 11.28).

To his prayer for strength, he had added a request for their stability. There is no point in something being strong if it is not stable. Interestingly, Paul specified that it was love, not knowledge, that would make the difference. There is always an interplay between our appreciation of Christ's love for us and our love for Him: "We love him, because he first loved us" (1 Jn 4.19).

Now his further request for them is for a more comprehensive understanding. The question is, a greater understanding of what? Some take it to refer to the divine love referred to in the following verse. However, in the context of the preceding verses his desire for them is probably broader, that they should share a multidimensional appreciation of the mysteries that had been revealed concerning the vastness of God's purposes for Christ, the Church, and the Christian. We may think of how broad God's plans are to bless all of His creation including Jew and Gentile. They are so long in that they were conceived in eternity past and will be on full display for all eternity to come. They are so deep as to require a Saviour to descend into death and die upon a cross. They are so high as to elevate sinners like ourselves and seat us with the glorified Christ above.

God's desire for us all is that our minds and hearts should keep on expanding.

3.19 - Spiritual Knowledge

**And to know the love of Christ, which passeth knowledge,
that ye might be filled with all the fulness of God.**

There are such wonderful heights to scale in Ephesians. We mere mortals can preach the unsearchable, grasp the immeasurable, and experience the unknowable! The Holy Spirit strengthens us, and now we learn that the love of Christ, God's Son, and the fulness of God, the Father, can be known. The full Godhead is active for our blessing.

The knowledge of the love of Christ is a practical or experiential knowledge. It is to be personally enjoyed day by day. How can this come about and how can it develop?

Christ can only be known through daily communion with Himself, as we read His Word, speak to Him in prayer, and walk through the day with Him. In the Scriptures we will learn more of Him and in the challenges of life we will enjoy more of His presence and help. We will find that He is the answer to our every need.

In Spurgeon's last sermon preached in the Metropolitan Tabernacle, London, on the 7th June, 1891, he said this: 'If you wear the livery of Christ you will find Him so meek and lowly of heart that you will find rest unto your souls. He is always to be found in the thickest part of the battle. When the wind blows cold He always takes the bleak side of the hill. The heaviest end of the cross lies ever on His shoulders. If He bids us carry a burden He carries it also.' Such companionship engenders the deepest love and affection for One so kind and tender. Christ's love surpasses knowledge in the sense that it is so vast and inexhaustible that we will never realise all of it or come to the end of it. We can know it now, but we will never know it fully. It is infinite.

Being filled with all the fulness of God is also to be realised in Christ, in whom dwells all the fulness of the Godhead (Col 2.9). This is progressive, literally "unto the fulness of God". Growth in godliness is the same as growth in Christlikeness. We will never be omnipotent or omniscient but we can be more loving, more gracious, more holy, and more faithful. Christ can be seen in us, and truth and godliness can mark us out as those who know Him.

When we spend time with Christ we become more like Him.

3.20 - An Outburst of Praise

Now unto him that is able to do exceeding abundantly above all that we ask or think, according to the power that worketh in us,

Paul's spirit was so stirred by the immensity of the truths he had been considering that he could not hold back from a spontaneous outburst of praise. This is what is known as a 'doxology', an ascription of glory to God, and there are other delightful examples of the same throughout the Scriptures. They almost catch us by surprise, and yet we are not surprised; we too can feel suddenly overwhelmed by the grace and goodness of our God. Such feelings thrill our souls and should be cherished.

It has often been noted how this short verse rises higher and higher, like a pinnacle. A graphic arrangement of the verse will imprint it upon our minds all the more firmly:

He is able
He is able to do
He is able to do exceeding
He is able to do exceeding abundantly
He is able to do exceeding abundantly above
He is able to do exceeding abundantly above all
He is able to do exceeding abundantly above all that we ask
He is able to do exceeding abundantly above all that we ask or think

We are not quite finished: all of the above is "according to the power that worketh in us". Our enablement has already been attributed to the indwelling Holy Spirit of God who continually helps and guides us.

As to the answering of our prayers, a word of caution is necessary. Our requests should be according to God's will and offered by us when we seek to be yielded and obedient to His Word: that is to say this verse is not a blank cheque for personal enrichment and luxurious living. There are those in Christendom today who urge their congregations to 'name it and claim it'. This provokes all kinds of hopes for buying a bigger car, landing a better job, or finding a rich spouse. God is not in the business of encouraging our selfishness (Jas 4.3). Apart from greed and worldliness, we may harbour in our hearts hidden and unconfessed sins. All of these things will hinder the workings of the Holy Spirit in our lives and short-circuit the flow of His power within us and through us (Ps 66.18).

In a tight corner it is good to remember that God is able.

3.21 - All Glory to Him

Unto him be glory in the church by Christ Jesus throughout all ages, world without end. Amen.

Bible scholars who study the ancient copies of the text suggest a different word order at this point, once again in an ascending fashion: 'in the Church (the body of Christ), and in Christ Jesus (the Head of the Church), let God be glorified'.

Only those who truly know God as their Father through faith in Christ are members of the Church which is His body. Corporately, in local church fellowship, they are to glorify God and honour His Son. The assembly gatherings of the Christians should always have this in mind. The weekly remembrance of Christ, when believers break the bread and drink from the cup, is a prime opportunity to praise and worship God. But every other meeting is an occasion for the same: when we gather to pray we cannot do so without praising Him; when we study His Word together we continue to find more and more reasons to give thanks and honour Him; when we preach the gospel from hearts overflowing with love we glorify Him, grateful for His amazing plan of recovery for a fallen creation.

In our personal lives too, we can begin every day by rejoicing in the Lord and being thankful for another opportunity to worship and serve Him: "I will praise thee, O Lord my God, with all my heart: and I will glorify thy name for evermore" (Ps 86.12). Every thought, word, and deed can be offered as sacrifices that please Him and bring glory to His Name.

If the Church through all eternity will show forth the manifold wisdom of God (Eph 3.10), then by the same measure it will ever be part of the heavenly choir ascribing glory to His Name. Bangor Abbey in Northern Ireland, dating from the fifth century, was reputed to have had a monastic choir whose 1,000 members served in three rotating shifts, praising God twenty-four hours a day for over 100 years. This was known as the *Laus Perennis* or 'perpetual praise'. Whatever the case, their voices have long been silent. Heaven will be so different. The Church will praise and glorify God unto all generations for ever and ever, and to this we can add our 'Amen'.

There is no higher occupation than to glorify God.

Chapter 4

Walk Straighter

Paul exhorts the Ephesians to holy living as those who are one in Christ.
Each believer has a gift that is to be used in love for the good of all, promoting growth and maturity, and each should have a clean testimony.

4.1-6   UNITY
4.7-16   DIVERSITY
4.17-32 SANCTITY

4.1 - A Worthy Walk

I therefore, the prisoner of the Lord, beseech you that ye walk worthy of the vocation wherewith ye are called,

The transition here from all that has gone before has been described in different ways: from riches to responsibilities, from doctrine to duty, from belief to behaviour, from wealth to walk etc. If we retain our picture of ascending to great heights we might describe the progression as being from heavenly blessedness to earthly usefulness. The lofty truths that Paul has described as to our exalted position in Christ must now be worked out in a practical way at ground level. Doctrine must never be separated from practice. The promises regarding the eternal future are to be appropriated and applied in this present temporal scene. Paul's use of the word 'therefore' is always significant. He never uses it without first having laid a firm foundation that gives authority to his appeal.

He reminded them of his imprisonment for the sake of the Lord. His mind had soared heavenwards, far beyond his confined circumstances, but he also had a heart for the Ephesian Christians who had to live out their faith in a challenging environment. It was as if he was coming right alongside them to issue his ongoing appeal, that their spiritual condition upon earth should perfectly complement their heavenly position in Christ. The God who is worthy of all glory expects His children to faithfully represent Him upon the earth.

Walking implies public testimony. It also implies constancy. One of the great examples from the Old Testament is Enoch, a man who walked with God for no less than 300 years (Gen 5.22). Without a Bible and without a local church to encourage him, this man nevertheless was able to enjoy daily and intimate communion with God on the pathway of life. This is the second of at least six references to walking in this epistle. Each has a particular emphasis: 2.10 walk diligently; 4.1 walk worthily; 4.17 walk purely; 5.2 walk lovingly; 5.8 walk truthfully; and 5.15 walk wisely.

The believer's calling has already been referred to (Eph 1.18) and it has in view the elevated position presently enjoyed as a result of having responded to the gospel call. It also includes the blessings to come when God's ultimate purposes for His children will be accomplished. This sense of God's intervention in our lives should produce in us an appropriate response of godly living in an ungodly world.

The pathway we walk should correspond to the profession we talk.

4.2 - A Gentle Spirit

With all lowliness and meekness, with longsuffering, forbearing one another in love;

This cluster of beautiful graces relates to our personal relationships. These were to mark the Christian community in their interactions with one another, as well as with the wider world. Harmony and civility are features of Christian testimony that speak volumes to unbelievers.

Humility is fragile and often in short supply. In the ancient world, it was generally regarded as an undesirable weakness of character. The ongoing challenge of those who had been Jews or those who had been Gentiles was to be Christlike in their attitude to one another. One can imagine a converted Jew still harbouring superior and condescending thoughts in his mind; 'I come from the line of God's specially chosen people. I will just have to learn to put up with these coarse and unschooled Gentiles.' The converted Gentile might develop a combative disposition: 'I am now just as good as any pompous Jew. I will show them what I am made of and knock them off their pedestal. Yes, and I will stand up for equal rights.' What both sides should have learnt from Paul's letter so far was that they were equally sinful and had been equally blessed with salvation on the principle of divine grace alone.

Gentleness accompanies humility. The One who came down from the highest place in heaven to assume the lowest place said, "I am meek and lowly in heart" (Mt 11.29). People who are driven by personal ambition can be forceful but inconsiderate of others. They certainly get things done by steamrolling all in their way, but they often leave behind them a trail of crushed and discouraged souls. Believers should not be 'driven' at all, but rather led by the Spirit. This will make all the difference to those who come into contact with them; they will be helped and not hindered.

Humility and gentleness produce patience, the short of patience that forbears with the weaknesses and shortcomings – not the sins – of others. Homes have been wrecked by harsh discipline that constantly pounced on the most minor infraction and never considered the need to positively encourage a spouse or children. Assemblies of Christians have also at times been torn apart by dominant and intolerant personalities who insisted on getting their own way, while claiming it was solely 'for truth's sake'.

These three graces are bound together with the essential component of love. Where would any of us be without the love of God that saw us in our need and bowed down to lift us up? How patient and gentle God continues to be with us all, His beloved children.

There can never be too much love among Christians.

4.3 - Unity

Endeavouring to keep the unity of the Spirit in the bond of peace.

The qualities found in the previous verse all come to bear on maintaining unity among the believers in a local church. Unity requires commitment and hard work. Paul's use of the words 'endeavour' and 'keep' imply this. It is an urgent priority that should never be neglected. It also needs the application of constant diligence lest that which is so precious is forfeited and lost.

It is the Holy Spirit of God who always promotes unity; those who are submissive to His leading and guiding will work to the same end. The perfect harmony in the Godhead is meant to inspire the same among the members of Christ's body.

Peace is the product when men and women are closely bound together as one in mutual love. Unity and peace together provide the fertile soil in which believers can grow, prosper and bear fruit for God. There is also positive reinforcement: if unity produces peace, then, in turn, peace will promote unity. Just as in a marriage, so in a local assembly, the initial commitment to remain together and go through all the ups and downs of life together develops over time into an inexplicable bond that grows stronger and stronger. A man and a woman find themselves knowing what each other is thinking; more often than not they voice the same opinion at exactly the same time. They have truly become "one flesh". Likewise, members of an assembly come to feel so much part of one another that they instinctively find themselves rejoicing with their brothers and sisters who have cause to rejoice, and weeping with those that weep (Rom 12.15).

The devil has become a master at dividing and ruling, both in the world and in the Church. The world has become increasingly fractious with everyone disagreeing with everyone else. While it is true that in the Church divisions have arisen over major issues of doctrine or morality, where there could be no compromise, it is also sad that at times much less important matters have set one believer against another. Those who claim to enjoy peace with God can at times scarcely say a kind word about their fellow-believers. What is described as being an important issue may be nothing more than a personality clash, a misunderstanding, or the result of a proud and unforgiving spirit. Whatever it is, the enemy rejoices.

"Blessed are the peacemakers." (Mt 5.9)

4.4 - Shared Blessings

There is one body, and one Spirit, even as ye are called in one hope of your calling;

From encouraging the Ephesian believers to consider one another and work hard to maintain harmony among themselves, Paul turned to remind them of seven unique features that they all share.

The one body referred to is the Church. This mystery has been revealed as God's purpose that Jew and Gentile should be united as one in the body of Christ and under His headship. While the Jew and Gentile issue is not prominent today, the truth remains that all people of all backgrounds have become part of that body through faith in Christ as Saviour and Lord.

The one Spirit is the Holy Spirit. On that day of Pentecost in Jerusalem, a unique baptism took place: the baptiser was Christ; the baptism was in the Spirit, not in water; and it was believers who were baptised into one body. That once-for-all baptism includes every child of God who from the moment of conversion is indwelt by the Holy Spirit. You and I were not present at Calvary and yet we have received the blessings that have come through the finished work of Christ. In the same way, although we were not present in Jerusalem on that day of Pentecost, we were included in all that took place then, and now we enjoy the rich spiritual blessings that have flowed from it. That is why Paul could write to the Corinthians believers and tell them "For by one Spirit are we all baptized into one body, whether we be Jews or Gentiles, whether we be bond or free; and have all been made to drink into one Spirit" (1 Cor 12.13). Some would teach that a person is saved first and then only later do they receive the Spirit. Paul refutes this: "Now if any man have not the Spirit of Christ, he is none of his" (Rom 8.9).

The one hope includes all that God has promised for His children in Christ: the hope of His calling (Eph 1.18); the hope of salvation (1 Thess 5.8); the hope of eternal life   (Tit 3.7); and the hope of glory (Col 1.27). There should be no doubt about any of these; they will all come to pass.

They cover the immediate blessings of salvation, the continued blessings of daily fellowship with Him, and the heavenly blessings yet to come.

All our hopes in Christ are sure and steadfast.

4.5 - Shared Responsibilities

One Lord, one faith, one baptism,

The Lordship of Christ is a prominent theme in Paul's writings. This was one of the first truths revealed to him when he met the Saviour on the Damascus Road. Saul of Tarsus, as he was then, had two questions: firstly, as to Christ's identity, "Who art thou, Lord?'; and secondly, as to Christ's authority, "Lord, what wilt thou have me to do?" (Acts 9.5-6). The answers to these questions shaped the rest of his life and ministry. The man, Jesus, he had so despised and whose followers he had so vehemently persecuted, was none other than Christ the Lord. From the first day of his conversion, Paul dedicated his whole being to furthering the interests of his Lord. He would go on to proclaim the Lord Jesus Christ far and near, to both Jew and Gentile, as the only Saviour.

In the first century, citizens of the Roman empire were expected to participate in an annual rite of taking a pinch of incense and casting it into a fire, proclaiming 'Caesar is Lord'. Christian believers owned allegiance to only one divine Lord to whom homage and worship were due. Their refusal to comply with the status quo aroused animosity; some suffered to the extent of being martyred for their faithfulness to Christ.

"One faith" can refer either to the act of believing in Christ or to the body of doctrine, the common foundation truths, that all Christians share and believe. The Scriptures make clear that there is only one way to be saved and that is to believe in Christ. Equally so, there can be no compromise on the apostolic doctrine that proclaims the absolute deity and sinless humanity of Christ, the sufficiency of His work upon the cross, the triumph of His resurrection, the glory of His ascension and exaltation, and the certainty of His coming again.

"One baptism" could refer to the baptism in the Holy Spirit on the day of Pentecost when the Church began (1 Cor 12.13), but the Ephesian believers would probably in the first instance recall their own baptism in water. This was the common and public act of confession by which believers then, as now, showed their obedience to Christ and their total identification with Him in His death, burial, and resurrection (Rom 6.3-6). On the day of Pentecost, those who had believed the gospel preached by Peter were baptised in water. About 3,000 souls were added to the church (Acts 2.41).

The Lord expects every believer to be baptised.

4.6 - Our God and Father

One God and Father of all, who is above all, and through all, and in you all.

The formulation of these three verses in this seven-fold way suggests that they could have been part of an early Christian confession.

The Fatherhood of God is a precious truth. He is not some remote figurehead, a dispassionate administrator, or even an absentee parent. He is a Father who loves every member of His family. He is pleased when He is at the centre of their lives and they gather around Him, staying close and listening to His every word. He cares for His children like no other, providing all that they need for as long as they need it, and protecting them for every danger. He is always available to give them the best personal advice and He will listen to their many problems and complaints. He is patient too with those who go astray; He is so loving that He does not overlook disciplining His erring children when they require it, but He never disowns any of them, even those that cause Him the most grief. The wayward nation of Israel dishonoured Him by doubting His love and despising His Name. God challenged them in this way: "A son honoureth his father ... if then I be a father, where is mine honour?" (Mal 1.6). In this present Church age we can know a holy intimacy with God that Israel never knew, and call Him "Abba, Father" (Rom 8.15; Gal 4.6).

God is above all in His preeminence. In sovereign majesty He transcends all of His creation. Before the worlds were made, He was there. He is "the high and lofty One that inhabiteth eternity, whose name is Holy" (Is 57.15).

God is through all in the outworking of His power. The Epistle to the Ephesians focuses on the divine purposes moving forward inexorably to their consummation. The world is in a chaotic state but the Christian can take heart that 'God is still on the throne, and He will remember His own.'

God's presence is in us all who have believed. He will never leave us, nor forsake us (Heb 13.5). Everyone born into His family will arrive safely home!

God has no favourites in His family – He loves every child equally.

4.7 - Gifted Believers

But unto every one of us is given grace according to the measure of the gift of Christ.

Having considered the unique features of the faith that all believers share, Paul now introduces the thought of individual gifts and their variety. Every believer has been given a special gift or ability that he or she can use for the blessing of those in the local church and also in the wider world. The proper use of these gifts reinforces unity.

Most emphasis is placed on public gifts. This is a mistake. A Spirit-directed and Spirit-enabled ministry of gospel preaching and Bible teaching is vital for the furtherance of God's work and the upbuilding of His people, but to focus on this is to miss the point. Every child of God, male or female, young or old, has a specific role to play, and often it is the quiet or unseen contribution that is the most vital and redolent with the fragrance of Christ.

This leads us to the admission that ability of itself is never enough. A humble attitude and pure motive must accompany it. Sometimes young men have been thrust into prominence and lauded for their public gift. Unless they are careful, they can become puffed up with pride; this will soon ruin their usefulness. As has been wisely remarked: 'Don't let praise go to your head or criticism get to your heart.' We can claim no merit for any gift that we have been given, but we will do well to be thankful for it, and be determined to develop and use it for God's glory and the blessing of others.

The bestowal of any particular gift is according to the overarching will of God. Here the thought is that Christ equips His disciples. In another scripture, it is the Holy Spirit that does so, "the selfsame Spirit, dividing to every man severally as he will" (1 Cor 12.11). In Romans 12, God is the giver (Rom 12.3). Again, complete harmony in the Godhead is evident. Christ provides exactly what we need with regard to our gift and its use. He does not expect us to do anything for Him without providing the resources to do it. It is not that God's grace is limited in its supply; keeping to the context, the point here is that He provides all that we require.

Have you used your gift today?

4.8 - Sharing the Spoils

**Wherefore he saith, When he ascended up on high,
he led captivity captive, and gave gifts unto men.**

Divine gifts have been dispensed to God's children by the risen, ascended and exalted Christ, the victorious One. Paul used an appropriate scripture quotation from Psalm 68, a Psalm of David. The background of the psalm is that of military conquest over the Philistines. In an earlier campaign, the Philistines had soundly defeated Israel and taken the ark of the covenant, the symbol of God's presence. They had lauded their victory and dominance by placing the ark in the temple of Dagon, their own heathen god, but were dismayed to find that the image of Dagon fell and was broken. Not only that, but also their menfolk were afflicted by serious illness. Motivated by fear, they soon returned the ark to the Israelites. Eventually, it was taken back to Jerusalem (returning to Jerusalem was always regards as an ascent) and placed once again in the innermost compartment of the tabernacle, the Holy of Holies. Paul linked this picture of triumph to Christ's exaltation. The victor received the spoils of battle (Ps 68.18) which were then shared with his army. Christ, the Conqueror, is now in heaven but He has gifted His Church with all that they need to carry on in His absence.

"He led captivity captive" can be understood in several ways. In either case, it alludes to a military leader returning from a successful military campaign. He takes the lead in the victory parade that welcomes him home. If the focus in this verse is on the vanquished army, then it can be viewed as a sorry reversal of their fortunes – they who once held others in captivity have now been captured themselves. If the focus is on the liberated ones, it is a picture of joy: they who once were under the thraldom of the enemy have now been gloriously set free and are under the rule of the liberator, or under 'new ownership' as we might say.

In Ephesians 2, sinners are seen as being under the bondage of the devil. Their captivity under this cruel despot was harsh and unyielding. In Christ they have been set free and have become willing servants to their Lord. This is a completely different kind of captivation: one of love and devotion. Paradoxically, it was through His death that Christ claimed the victory, destroying him that had the power of death, that is, the devil, and delivering those who through fear of death had been subject to bondage (Heb 2.14-15).

We are on the victory side!

4.9 - Christ's Descent

(Now that he ascended, what is it but that he also descended first into the lower parts of the earth?

This and the next verse are a parenthesis, or insertion, emphasising that Christ who ascended had first descended. This main point is clear enough but a great deal of discussion has centred on explaining the meaning of "the lower parts of the earth". When we face a difficult verse like this, how should we proceed? The following principles may assist us:

1. Keep clear in your mind what you do understand: Christ descended then ascended.
2. Admit what you do not understand: the meaning of "the lower parts of the earth".
3. Read the passage in its context over and over again, and form a tentative opinion.
4. Read different translations and other Bible verses that shed further light.
5. Consult books and commentaries giving the opinions of different scholars.
6. Consider their arguments carefully and continue to pray for guidance.
7. Revise your own opinion (see no. 3 above) if necessary.
8. Do not fall out with anyone who may think differently.

The main options for this verse would seem to fall into three groups: the phrase may simply mean this earth below the heavens; it may refer to the death and burial of the Lord Jesus; or it might also be a reference to hades (the Old Testament *sheol*), the place of departed spirits. Each view has its advocates and each view has its difficulties. You may be dismayed to discover that some commentaries seem to skip the difficult passages. (We have tried not to do so throughout this volume.)

It is most likely a reference to death and the grave, or in other words, the depths of shame and suffering into which Christ entered. These have been answered by the heights of exaltation and glory which He has now attained. This view would accord with the teaching of Paul in his letter to the Philippians (Phil 2.7-8): the downward path of Christ in humbling Himself and dying at the hands of sinners has been followed by God's response in exalting and honouring His Son.

We rejoice that Christ came down to earth and went down into death for us.

4.10 – Christ's Ascent

He that descended is the same also that ascended up far above all heavens, that he might fill all things.)

The depths into which Christ entered have been matched by the heights to which He has returned. We tend to think geographically, which may not always be the sense of Scripture when referring to spiritual truth about divine Persons. However, the Scriptures speak of Christ going up, being taken up, ascending up, and being received up (as already considered in Eph 1.20).

The realm of the heavens is conveniently explained by thinking of three spheres: the terrestrial or earthly heavens directly above us, where the birds fly; the celestial heavens beyond that, where the stars are; and the eternal heavens, the third heaven, where God dwells. The apostle Paul recalled an extraordinary event in his life when he was "caught up to the third heaven ... into paradise, and heard unspeakable words, which it is not lawful for a man to utter" (2 Cor 12.2-4).

Christ has ascended "far above all heavens". We would all agree that He deserves the highest place there is. The Christian, living as he or she does in a world of chaos, confusion and evil, will do well to keep the thought of the exalted Christ prominent in the mind and heart.

One of God's purposes in the exaltation of Christ is that He might fill the universe. This goes beyond the truth of divine omnipresence. It encompasses also His glory and rule which will be manifested to all, everywhere and throughout eternity. It has pleased the Father that in Christ all fulness should dwell (Col 1.19), and as Paul reaffirmed to the Colossians, "in him dwelleth all the fulness of the Godhead bodily" (Col 2.9). At the end of the first chapter of Ephesians, it was noted that fulness is linked to the Church which is His body (Eph 1.23).

The movements of Christ are all marked by grace and glory. His love brought Him down to meet us in our need, so that we, who were 'sunk in ruin, sin, and misery', could be lifted up. Thank God, the One who went down into suffering, death and shame for us is now the exalted One. We bow at His feet and worship.

> Behold the Lamb with glory crowned,
> To Him all pow'r is giv'n:
> No place too high for Him is found,
> No place too high in heaven.
>
> Thomas Kelly

4.11 - Gifts to the Church

And he gave some, apostles; and some, prophets; and some, evangelists; and some, pastors and teachers;

Christ's gifts to the Church are people with spiritual abilities to perform different essential roles. The first two of the five mentioned here were necessary for the early Church but no longer function today. The other three continue to this day and are vital for the growth and development of the Church.

Apostles and prophets have already been mentioned in their role of establishing the early Church (Eph 2.20). Apostles had been personally commissioned by the Lord and they testified to Him as being the foundation rock of the Church. Prophets in the time of the early Church received appropriate and timely instruction from heaven and conveyed it to the first Christians. Both of these roles were necessary before the New Testament was written. When the Bible was complete, however, God's full revelation to His children then became their one and only guide. It remains the same today.

For the Church to grow, the message of the gospel has to be proclaimed everywhere. The first Christians were bold to witness to all they came into contact with concerning their Saviour. Even when they fled persecution and were scattered abroad, they did not refrain from boldly witnessing (Acts 8.4). The Lord called and raised up men who were especially gifted to preach the gospel wherever they went. These were known as evangelists, the proclaimers of God's good news. They devoted their full time to this task and travelled extensively.

New converts had to be cared for and taught the Word of God. That is why God gave other gifts to the Church. The pastors (also known as elders or overseers) were men with shepherd hearts whom God raised up to feed, guide, and protect the believers. They would tend their flock and provide for their every need. A number of these men functioned together in each local assembly. Theirs was not an itinerant ministry but rather a fixed, local responsibility. While they were all to be capable of teaching the Word (1 Tim 3.2), they had many other responsibilities and demands on their time. Another specific gift God gave to the Church were men who devoted their lives to teaching the Word. Not all of these were elders in a local assembly; some would travel from place to place, but always to build up the believers with instruction in the Word.

Do you know who your shepherds are?
Do you pray for them regularly by name?

4.12 – Fully Equipped

**For the perfecting of the saints, for the work of the ministry,
for the edifying of the body of Christ:**

The different ministries of gospel preaching, Bible teaching, and shepherding all combine to fully equip believers in their growth and service, so that Christ can use them effectively for every good work (2 Tim 2.21). As we have noted, there is a wide range of gifts given to the Church, but the ones Paul specifically mentions here are the more public gifts.

The idea of perfection as normally understood is not found in this verse. The word 'perfect' in the New Testament usually means mature; just here it means to be fully equipped or furnished. There is no such thing as a sinlessly perfect believer and no such thing as a perfect assembly of Christians. The letters of the New Testament written to various churches, including the letters to the seven churches in the book of Revelation, make this clear.

Gifts are not an end in themselves, just as salvation is not an end in itself. We are saved so that we might serve God and His people, and our gifts are given to us to be used for the good and blessing of others. We are to be channels of blessing, not end-points. The glory that accrues is not to boost the one who has the gift but to honour the Lord whom he serves.

Equipping the saints requires that they are taught the Word of God, by example as well as by word of mouth. The goal is not solely that they become more knowledgable about the Scriptures. Knowledge of itself can cause believers to be puffed up with pride, but the truth of God's Word needs to be built into their character and worked out in their lives, so that they become more like Christ and honour Him in service.

Every local church should make the teaching of the Scriptures a priority. Spiritual food, in a balanced diet of 'milk' for the young in the faith and 'meat' for the more mature, should be on the menu at all times. A systematic and comprehensive programme of Bible instruction for all the saints requires simplicity and consistency. And yet Paul had a broader perspective here, beyond the limits of a local assembly. He was taking the panoramic view of the whole body of Christ, being built up strong and true.

God's servants are to be men and women of the Book.

4.13 – More like Christ

Till we all come in the unity of the faith, and of the knowledge of the Son of God, unto a perfect man, unto the measure of the stature of the fulness of Christ:

Paul is taking the saints higher and higher. Gifts have been given to be a blessing to others and also to build up the Church until the whole body will be complete. Spiritual growth is a process that keeps in focus that coming day when we shall be fully conformed to Christ Himself.

Those who are bound together in one body are to grow together. They share the same truth but they also love the same things, they work towards the same goals, and they honour the same Lord. They feel part of one another and are bonded together by genuine mutual concern and care for one another. Their unity is visibly expressed by how they live together in harmony, as much as by their profession of doctrinal agreement. The Lord said to His disciples, "By this shall all men know that ye are my disciples, if ye have love one to another" (Jn 13.35).

The 'knowledge' of Christ, the Son of God, again takes us beyond merely reading and learning about the Lord Jesus from the Scriptures. This is an experimental knowledge that comes from enjoying daily communion with Him. When we stay close to Him we learn of Him: we walk as He walks, we speak as He speaks, and we act as He acts.

We are to become more mature as individuals and as a body of believers growing together in conformity to the Head. There is a great delight in seeing a young child develop and achieve its milestones. However, there is always a concern when this growth appears to be arrested. Appropriate behaviour at the age of two would be inappropriate ten years later. Godly shepherds have a concern for the progress and spiritual development of each member of the flock under their care.

The high point, as we have mentioned before, is to become more like Christ, here and now. The outshining of Christlikeness brings blessing wherever it is seen. We all would admit to failure along the way, but we have a sure and certain hope that one day we shall be fully and completely like Him (1 Jn 3.2).

"Is Jesus Christ like you?"
(The question an African chief asked a missionary.)

4. 14 - Stability

That we henceforth be no more children, tossed to and fro, and carried about with every wind of doctrine, by the sleight of men, and cunning craftiness, whereby they lie in wait to deceive;

Having considered the goals of unity, maturity and ultimate conformity to Christ, Paul brings us back to the here and now by addressing the potential problems of immaturity and instability. In descriptive language, reminding us of a storm at sea, he depicts the spiritually immature as being unstable and vulnerable to every doctrinal error swirling around in the wind. They are also prey to evil deceivers who are deliberately waiting for the right opportunity to blow them off course.

The word 'children' is used here in a negative way to describe believers who have not grown and developed spiritually as they ought to have. They were somewhat like the Hebrews who should have been able to feed on the meat of the Word but remained at the milk stage (Heb 5.12).

Paul's language describes the situation among the Ephesians as he saw it then. There were immature believers among them, and he was calling for them to grow up.

In other Scriptures the word 'children' is used in a positive sense as a term of affection (2 Cor 6.13; Gal 4.19; 1 Jn 2.1), or as an encouragement to portray the family characteristics of the children of God: "Ye are all the children of light" (1 Thess 5.5); "As obedient children, not fashioning yourselves according to the former lusts in your ignorance" (1 Pet 1.14). The apostle Peter's exhortation that the saints should be "as newborn babes", desiring "the sincere milk of the word" (1 Pet 2.2), referred to the necessary thirst that every child of God should have for the Word of God.

The reality Paul identifies in this verse is that there are men who are dangerous and devious, who pretend to be teachers of the truth but who are in fact disseminators of gross error. They act deliberately with malicious intent to deceive believers.

In the light of these dangers, there is a great need for every one of us to read our Bibles daily to learn more of God's ways and be careful about other books and magazines we may read. We also need to be taught the truth by faithful and godly men of sound reputation. We should not be careless, either, about attending the local assembly of Christians where we gather. It is the truth that sets us free; error leads to bondage.

May we all grow in grace and in the knowledge of our Lord Jesus Christ.

4.15 – Charity

But speaking the truth in love, may grow up into him in all things, which is the head, even Christ:

Charity, or love, is a distinguishing Christian virtue. God is love, His Son was always motivated by love, and His disciples are to be marked by the same selfless, sacrificial and unconditional love.

This verse is dealing with how we live as well as what we say. To speak one thing but live another is hypocrisy. There is no conflict between truth and love. They are inseparable, and any suggestion that one can exist without the other is a distortion. Without love, any expression of the truth will be harsh and ineffective. Without truth, love becomes little more than indulgent sentimentality. The motives of the devious false teachers were to spread error and do harm to God's children. The motives of the godly in all of their conversation would be to uphold truth and do good to God's children so that they will be blessed.

The goal of maturity is that we should grow up spiritually to be like our Head, the Lord Jesus Christ. This will be a lifetime process. Admirers of newborn babies and infants are often heard making such comments as 'he has his father's eyes' or 'she has her mother's hair'. After a few years have passed additional comparisons might be made: 'he walks like his father' or 'she talks like her mother'. What has happened is that with the growth of the child, other characteristics have come to light.

Our goal should ever be that we become more and more like Christ, and that our lives should be lost in His. That is not to say that our distinctive personalities will disappear, but that He will be seen more clearly in us. The apostle Paul summed it up when he declared "For to me to live is Christ" (Phil 1.21).

It has always been remarked that when you spend a lot of time with someone else and admire them, you tend to become like them. This happens unconsciously (2 Cor 3.18). May it be that day by day, as we walk and talk with our blessed Saviour, that His beauty will be reflected in our lives, and that others might take note that we have "been with Jesus" (Acts 4.13). One day that likeness will be complete!

And is it so! we shall be like Thy Son?
Is this the grace which He for us has won?
Father of glory! (thought beyond all thought)
In glory to His own blest likeness brought.

J. N. Darby

4.16 - Joined Together

From whom the whole body fitly joined together and compacted by that which every joint supplieth, according to the effectual working in the measure of every part, maketh increase of the body unto the edifying of itself in love.

Christ, the Head, oversees the growth of the body which is His Church and provides all that it needs to function. Once again the truth of unity is emphasised, for what use are the limbs of a body unless they are joined together? It is Christ who assigns the particular place of each member in His body and knits all of them together. Just as ligaments and their associated blood vessels hold a limb in its proper place and provide the nutrients it needs, so Christ nourishes the individual members with His own life.

The body only grows, or is built up, in love. The harmonious functioning of every part together requires that each responds to the instructions from the Head, and that each assists the other in carrying out those instructions.

One dark night, many years ago, I came across a serious road accident in Gaborone and stopped to offer some help. A man had been crossing the main road from a hotel and was struck by a vehicle which did not stop. He was in a serious condition, bleeding profusely. His legs had been completely severed from his body. One limb was discovered later by the kerbside, further down the road, but the other was never found. The man passed away soon afterwards.

This sad and shocking event underlines a solemn truth that we often overlook. Each of us has a function in the body of Christ and in the local assembly of Christians where we gather (which functions like a body). We can only fulfil that function if we are together, not only physically but also spiritually. The first Christians gathered in Jerusalem and it is said of them that "they were all with one accord in one place" (Acts 2.1).

To treat local church attendance casually shows that we little understand the significance of the truth Paul is patiently unfolding. How can a body function with absent members? To attend church gatherings but be at odds with other believers is a similar affront to our Saviour. How can we function properly together if we disagree with one another?

God grant us the grace to honour Christ, our Head,
and to love each other.

4.17 - Not as Others

This I say therefore, and testify in the Lord, that ye henceforth walk not as other Gentiles walk, in the vanity of their mind,

The exhortation here follows on from that given at the beginning of the chapter where Paul encouraged the believers to walk worthy of their calling. Their manner of life was to be completely different manner from what it used to be; they had once "walked according to the course of this world, according to the prince of the power of the air" (Eph 2.2).

The difference in a transformed life speaks volumes to others. It is only then than our words of testimony will carry real weight. And if there is something in our lives that is contrary to what we profess, then we need not be surprised if others reject our attempts to witness to them. It will never work.

Paul makes clear that this exhortation goes far beyond a personal idea of his: this was the mind of the Lord as revealed to Him and faithfully passed on to the believers. On other occasions he used the same sort of language, for example, when he was advising the Corinthians about marriage problems. Concerning celibacy, he wrote "I speak this by permission, and not of commandment", whereas concerning a husband and wife remaining together he said, "unto the married I command, yet not I, but the Lord, Let not the wife depart from her husband" (1 Cor 7.6, 10). The first was a personal preference; the second was a divine command as taught by the Lord Himself. However, both are now part of the inspired Word of God and should be given careful consideration.

The Gentiles of those times were steeped in idolatry and this was often linked with gross immorality. We recall that temple prostitution was prevalent in Ephesus. Despite the claims of those who say mankind has progressed beyond religious beliefs and practices, all the evidence shows that little has changed. The idols of today may look different, but nevertheless, men's minds and hearts are focused on everyone and everything except the true and living God. They live for the material things of this world, forgetting that these will all be left behind and eventually pass away. The strange thing is that when men and women of today desire something more than the material, they often reach out to the occult. In effect, they are turning back to the superstitious practices that marked the first century. So much for progress!

Do not be afraid to stand out and be different, for Christ's sake.

4.18 - Darkness

**Having the understanding darkened,
being alienated from the life of God through the ignorance that
is in them, because of the blindness of their heart:**

Darkness, alienation, ignorance and blindness are a serious indictment of the condition of men and women who are at a distance from God, having turned away from Him.

It is important to understand that although every son and daughter of Adam is born with a sinful nature, God has revealed the truth about Himself to all mankind including the Gentiles: "For the invisible things of him from the creation of the world are clearly seen, being understood by the things that are made, even his eternal power and Godhead; so that they are without excuse: Because that, when they knew God, they glorified him not as God, neither were thankful; but became vain in their imaginations, and their foolish heart was darkened" (Rom 1.20-21). When God's light is rejected, darkness falls.

Alienation from God and ignorance are a direct result of a deliberate choice: "And even as they did not like to retain God in their knowledge, God gave them over to a reprobate mind" (Rom 1.28). Romans 1 also repeats the fact that men perversely changed God's truth into a lie and changed God's order into complete disorder. Such persistent refusal and rejection of the love, light, and life of God lead to hardening of the heart.

The pharaoh in Moses' time had many opportunities to respond positively to the word of the Lord. He hardened his heart wilfully, and later God hardened his heart judicially (Ex 8.32; 9.12). It is a fearful thing to resist the truth and it is possible for believers, not just unconverted sinners, to do the same. The conscience can become seared when the voice of the Holy Spirit within is continually being silenced. Soon, things that once troubled us are accommodated, without any apparent regret or a second thought.

The writer to the Hebrews appealed to his readers to respond to the voice of God: "To day if ye will hear his voice, harden not your hearts, as in the provocation" (Heb 3.15). The 'provocation' was that period in the wilderness when the children of Israel complained about God's ways, His provision, and even His protection. Their hearts were in a state of rebellion and God judged them accordingly. None of those who left Egypt entered Canaan, except Joshua and Caleb, and it was all because of unbelief (Heb 3.19).

A tender conscience before God is a strength, not a weakness.

4.19 - Uncleanness

Who being past feeling have given themselves over unto lasciviousness, to work all uncleanness with greediness.

To the sad catalogue of features marking sinners in their distance from God, is added signs of their further degradation. They become so insensitive and callous that they lose the ability to distinguish right from wrong. Sin no longer pains or troubles them in any way. With total abandon they follow after every kind of immorality. They are also unrestrained in desiring what belongs to others and seeking to acquire it for themselves. The implication is that they will resort to any means to do so.

It is interesting again to contrast what we have here with Paul's teaching in the first chapter of Romans. Here it is sinners who give themselves over to sin. In Romans, Paul mentions that God gave them up and gave them over to their chosen way of living (Rom 1.24, 26, 28) In other words, after they rejected His truth, he allowed them to have what they desired. Their choices had inevitable consequences.

Lasciviousness is a word we do not use much, if at all, in everyday language. It refers to all kinds of immorality. Living as we do in a world awash with sexual imagery and obsessed with gratuitous and self-indulgent relationships outside of marriage, the dangers are just as prevalent today as they were in the first century. The media seem to thrive on reporting the latest scandal. Pressure groups seek to control the conversation relating to what is legal and what is regarded as morally good. They persistently lobby for their personal right to live as they please and have society regard it as normal. And yet, the Word of God stands unchanged. It must continue to be our only guide through the darkness of this world.

It may seem strange to link covetousness, as the word means here, with the gross evil already mentioned. While many will deny ever breaking a number of the ten commandments such as murder or adultery, most would confess to having had feelings of covetousness at one time or another. Theft, violent robbery, fraud and embezzlement, all arise from the common root of covetousness. Paul will have more to say about it before he ends his letter.

In a world marked by unholiness and greed,
Christians are to be pure and kind.

4.20 - Learning Christ

But ye have not so learned Christ;

From all that marks the world and its evil ways, a great contrast is presented. It is the Christ who has made all the difference to the believer. While it is important to know more of His teaching, this cannot be divorced from getting to know Him personally. The closer we are to Him, the more separate we will be from the world and its sin.

We have only to view the heights of His love and the depths of His grace, to feel overwhelmed with God's goodness to us through His Son. He lived in complete obedience to His Father's will; no blot of wilful sin or selfish indulgence ever stained that holy and consecrated life. In the prime of manhood, He poured out His life for us in death so that we could be rescued from the ravages of sin and the terrible consequences of eternal punishment. He faced the battle alone so that we could be reconciled back to God.

Learning Christ is based firstly on us coming to know Him and, applying these verses to our own lives (vv. 20-24), Paul reminds us of our new position in Him. We first fled to Him as our Saviour, His arms outstretched in welcome. Relieved to know that our sins were forgiven and we had now become possessors of eternal life, we began to walk and talk with Him. We also began to understand that He is meant to be Lord of all. He said to His stumbling and gaffe-prone group of lowly disciples: "Take my yoke upon you, and learn of me; for I am meek and lowly of heart: and ye shall find rest unto your souls" (Mt 11.29). He is such a patient teacher with us who are so dull of spiritual hearing and dim of spiritual vision.

As we travel on the journey of life there are times when we face challenges and difficulties that we never could have anticipated. The storms assail us and the waves threaten to overcome us. It is then that we realise we are not alone. He has never left us and is right beside us; He is able by His mighty arm to bring us safely through.

Learning Christ is a lifetime process of getting to know Him better through the daily reading His Word, through speaking to Him often in prayer, and through His constant companionship in the ups and downs of life.

Christ is the most patient teacher and the most faithful friend.

4.21 - Taught by Christ

But if so be that ye have heard him, and have been taught by him, as the truth is in Jesus:

Christ teaches by example as well as by precept. Dr Luke in writing to his friend, Theophilus, referred to his first gospel volume as a "treatise ... of all that Jesus began both to do and teach" (Acts 1.1). The first is as important as the second and would encourage us to walk with Him, as well as listen to Him. Like ourselves, the Ephesian believers had never actually seen Him or heard Him but they were to regard the teaching of the apostle and others as coming directly to them from the risen Lord.

It is unusual for Paul to use Christ's earthly family name, 'Jesus', in isolation. When the Lord spoke to His disciples and told them, "I am the way, the truth, and the life" (Jn 14.6), He was affirming that in manhood He was the embodiment and source of all that was true, as well as being the only way to life. Sinners could only come to the Father by Him.

This holy intimacy with Christ is often missing from our lives. We attend Bible teaching meetings and go away thinking more of how the teacher fared – was he good or not so good? Was he better than the other speaker the previous week? These are the inconsequential issues that engage us rather than the central question we should all be asking – what has the Lord been saying to me today through His Word? We fill our lives with such distractions and frequently miss the main point.

Christ taught simply, using illustrations and objects from everyday life. His teaching was intimate and pointed. While there are good reasons to use and benefit from what is described today as 'expository preaching', a verse-by-verse explanation of a passage of Scripture in its context (as attempted in this volume), the gospel records have but few examples of the Lord using this approach when He referred to the Old Testament scriptures, the Bible of His day. It is also interesting that when He was with His disciples in the upper room in Jerusalem, His teaching on the Holy Spirit is recorded as being a line or two here and a line or two there. We are left to bring the threads together ourselves.

All of us have a lifetime enrolment in the 'school' of Christ.

4.22 - The Old Man

That ye put off concerning the former conversation the old man, which is corrupt according to the deceitful lusts;

What should be the effect of Christ's teaching? Paul here affirms that the purpose of His instruction is to effect a complete change in our way of life.

The "old man" is all that we were as sons of Adam, with our sinful nature and fleshly desires. On trusting Christ, the sinner is placed in a new position under the headship of Christ. He is regarded as having died with Christ, been buried and raised with Him, and walking in newness of life. Baptism in water is a picture of this new position (Rom 6.3-4).

While conversion brings a dramatic change as to our position, this must continue to be worked out in daily living and manifested in our spiritual condition. Old habits sometimes cling to us. Yes, many quickly divest themselves of more obvious aspects of a worldly lifestyle – they no longer visit old haunts to spend an evening drinking with former friends – but that is not the whole story. Other elements of character such as impatience, bad temper, selfishness and pride, do not disappear overnight. They are like old familiar clothing we have worn for so long that we regard them as part of us. They too must be discarded.

Sin will always appear attractive to the flesh, but "deceitful lusts" promise satisfaction and fulfilment that they can never deliver. This is the devil's master plan: millions are chasing the wind but will never catch it. King Solomon had the opportunity to put to the test the human quest for riches, worldly pleasure and more, as a means to satisfaction. He concluded that all such quests proved to be empty and vain (Eccl 12.8). Even believers can sometimes fool themselves into thinking that they are missing some vital joy that can be found only in the world. We need to settle the matter in our minds and hearts – the root of sin is selfishness, and the fruit is always shame, sorrow, and death.

There will always be tension between our position in Christ and our spiritual condition. With the Lord's help, any gap in this respect can be closed. It will require a daily and lifetime commitment to seek to be obedient to God's Word and to be honest with ourselves. While self-judgment is vital, keeping close company with the Lord will inevitably mould us and transform us to become more like Him.

Let us not dress in the rags of sin.

4.23 - A Change of Mind

And be renewed in the spirit of your mind;

The importance of the mind and heart cannot be overemphasised. In the New Testament, they are closely linked as the seat of reason and desire. Conversion is linked with repentance, and repentance by definition is a change of mind and heart. What begins at conversion is to continue throughout life. The renewal here refers to the frequent readjustments we must all make to align our thinking more closely and more fully with the Word of God and the mind of Christ (1 Cor 2.16).

Significantly, it is not merely the human mind that requires to be renewed but Paul says "the spirit of your mind". This refers to our spiritual perception and appreciation of our relationship to God, our riches in His Son, and our responsibilities to live to please Him. We have the Holy Spirit within our hearts, as it were, and the Holy Scriptures in our hands. These promote our spiritual renewal and revival. We should read our Bibles regularly. When we do, the Holy Spirit prompts us to obey.

Paul expands the thought in Romans 12 where he appeals to the believers in this way: "And be not conformed to this world: but be ye transformed by the renewing of your mind, that ye may prove what is that good, and acceptable, and perfect, will of God" (Rom 12.2). He did not want them to be shaped or moulded by the world and its values; rather, his desire for them was that their minds should be continually renewed to appreciate God's will for their lives, and be motivated to fulfil it. This is the ongoing radical transformation that we all need.

The world wages war to control our minds. The relentless bombardment by the media does us more harm than we care to admit. That is why we need a sanctuary, a quiet place and a daily quiet time to read God's Word, and to think and pray. Our study of the Christian's armour, as Paul describes it in this letter, still awaits us (Eph 6.10-17). For now, we may note that a helmet is needed to protect our minds and a sword is needed to defend us.

How often do we need to be renewed? As suggested above, this is best viewed as being a vital daily exercise for us all. Just as we renew our physical strength by eating food every day, so our spiritual health depends upon regular nourishment.

There is a battle for our minds. Only God can give us the victory.

4.24 - The New Man

And that ye put on the new man, which after God is created in righteousness and true holiness.

While it is important to divest ourselves of all that characterised us as sinners, we are not to be 'unclothed'. In fact, we need to be well-dressed Christians, exhibiting the features of our new nature and all that we are in Christ. God, who created the wonderful universe, is still at work in us creating something beautiful for His glory. "Therefore if any man be in Christ, he is a new creature [creation]: old things are passed away; behold, all things are become new" (2 Cor 5.17). While there is much discussion in trying to define exactly the meaning of "the new man", the thrust of it includes the change in our position before God as being under the headship of Christ, as well as the change in our condition before men.

The outward evidence of the change should be apparent to all. The beauty of Christ, His righteousness and holiness, should be seen in us. The meaning of these two words is closely related. We might think of one emphasising the positive – doing what is right, and the other reminding us too of the negative side – refraining from doing anything that is wrong. But there is much more involved because the root idea of holiness is being separated unto God. It is as a consequence of positively seeking after Him that we separate ourselves from other things that are sinful and would hinder our communion with Him. While at conversion we are justified, God declares us righteous, and also set apart for God as saints, the rest of our lives require us to show out what we are. These are practical truths.

A similar passage in Colossians details many more items of 'clothing', all covered with an overcoat of love: "Put on therefore ... bowels of mercies, kindness, humbleness of mind, meekness, longsuffering; Forbearing one another, and forgiving one another ... And above all these things put on charity, which is the bond of perfectness" (Col 3.12-14).

The imperative command shows that we are responsible before God to make the right choices as to how we live before Him. He has provided for us all that we need to honour Him; He has given us His Son, His Spirit and the Holy Scriptures. However, the deep-seated root of selfishness remains, and the flesh is always seeking an opportunity to control us. The world is all around, and the devil is working overtime to stumble us. May we choose well today.

The 'well-dressed' Christian looks like Christ.

4.25 - Speaking Truth

Wherefore putting away lying, speak every man truth with his neighbour: for we are members one of another.

Paul turns to address plain and practical matters that concern us all. One of the effects of following Christ should be that we no longer tell lies. This applies to all our dealings with others, whoever they may be, but it has a special significance among a fellowship of believers who profess to be bound together in love. We need to be able to trust one another, therefore honesty and transparency should characterise us at all times.

Lying is endemic in all societies. When Paul wrote to Titus to strengthen him for the task ahead in establishing the Christian testimony on the island of Crete, he quoted Epimenides, one of their poets, who was bold enough to declare that "The Cretians are alway liars, evil beasts, slow bellies" (Tit 1.12). Appropriately, at the beginning of his letter to Titus, Paul had reminded him of the God who cannot lie (Tit 1.2). Satan, by contrast, is described as the father of lies, and the Lord Jesus described the scheming Pharisees as being his children (Jn 8.44).

From Genesis through to Revelation the Bible is full of examples of people who have sought to deceive others. Lies can be direct and blatant; they can also be more subtle and nuanced, or even elaborate and premeditated. We think of old, dim-eyed Isaac asking his son Jacob, "Who are thou, my son? And Jacob said unto his father, I am Esau thy firstborn ... Art thou my very son Esau? And he said, I am" (Gen 27.18, 24). In another shameful incident, after Joseph's brothers had sold him, they planned their deception by taking his coat and dipping it in the blood of a young goat they had killed. Returning to their father they said to him, "This have we found: know now whether it be thy son's coat or no" (Gen 37.32).

In the early Church, the sad story of Ananias and Sapphira stands as a warning to us all. They had wanted to impress others by pretending they had presented the full proceeds of a land sale for the Lord's work when instead they had kept back some for themselves. Judgment was swift and severe (Acts 5.1-11). Any assembly of Christians should be marked by transparency and accountability in regard to finances. Wise and godly elders will make it their business to keep the saints regularly informed about the use of assembly funds.

To know Christ is to know the Truth.

4.26 - Anger Management

Be ye angry, and sin not: let not the sun go down upon your wrath:

This verse is not an encouragement to be angry. What it means is that when we are angry, we must be careful that the anger does not escalate into malicious thoughts, words, or deeds. We should also seek to resolve the issue, at least in our own minds and hearts, so that we do not end the day in emotional turmoil.

Paul was quoting directly from the Septuagint, the Greek version of the Old Testament, where in Psalm 4.4 the text says, "Tremble and do not sin". This is a reminder that the emotion of anger can cause physical changes: increased heart rate, rising blood pressure, heightened facial colour, and even shaking of the head or body. We say, 'He looked as if he was about to explode', or 'She was ready to boil over'.

Being angry is not necessarily sinful. A holy God can be righteously angry (Deut 9.8, 20; Ps 7.11). As for ourselves, there are good reasons for us feeling outraged when we hear of some heinous crime committed against innocent victims. In other words, we can be angry at the same things that anger God. There are other reasons for being angry that are not so easily justified. When proud people feel offended at not getting their own way, they are often incensed and begin plotting some means of retaliation.

Unresolved anger is dangerous, especially to interpersonal relationships. Among Christians, it has the potential to divide marriages, families, and assemblies of believers. Simmering resentments and longstanding grudges do more harm to the offended party as to anyone else. With the passage of time these harboured feelings become like a festering wound that completely poisons both mind and heart.

How then are we to manage our anger? It helps to pause before responding – some people count to ten – and say as little as possible. An emergency 'arrow prayer', such as Nehemiah sent heavenwards (Neh 6.14), is an acknowledgment that we cannot cope on our own. We will need to humble ourselves and talk it over with the Lord, bringing it before Him and telling Him how we feel. But then, we will need to listen and allow Him to answer us. He will put things into perspective and remind us of where our anger could lead. He will guide us as to what we should do.

"A soft answer turneth away wrath." (Prov 15.1)

4.27 - Resisting the Devil

Neither give place to the devil.

Lying, anger, and the devil are a toxic mix. We can be quickly overcome by all of these. Constant vigilance is required and the devil must not be allowed to gain a foothold. Once he has done so, he will advance rapidly in his goal of complete domination.

The devil is the relentless enemy of our souls. He has already been identified in this letter as "the prince of the power of the air" (Eph 2.2). He will reappear later as a wily adversary and the wicked one (Eph 6.11, 16). His power, guile, and evil intent should not be underestimated. He is like an angel of light in his subterfuge, like a lion constantly on the prowl, and like a dragon in his ferocity. In the Garden of Eden, he appeared to Eve as a deceiving serpent.

The word 'devil' means a slanderer. The word 'satan means an adversary. Foiled in his initial attempt to usurp God (Is 14.12-15; Ezek 28.2, 17), the devil was cast down from heaven to lower realms. Since then he has constantly opposed God's purposes for mankind upon the earth. As far as you and I are concerned as believers, he wants to ruin us and boast of our downfall. He will use deception and guile as well as direct frontal attacks; he knows our individual weaknesses and will exploit them to the full.

It is helpful to remember that he is already a defeated foe. At Calvary the Lord Jesus gained the victory, having first taken upon Himself flesh and blood, "that through death he might destroy him that had the power of death, that is, the devil; And deliver them who through fear of death were all their lifetime subject to bondage" (Heb 2.14-15). The devil's stranglehold has been broken, but he is still active and unceasing in his attempts to spoil all that God would purpose. James gave good advice: "Resist the devil, and he will flee from you" (Jas 4.7).

The devil is described elsewhere as "the god of this world" (2 Cor 4.4) who is still blinding the minds of those who do not believe the gospel; he is seeking to prevent them from coming to the light and knowing the blessing of God. His final defeat and judgment lie ahead when he and his emissaries will be cast into the lake of fire where they will be punished for ever and ever (Rev 20.10).

Satan never sleeps.

4.28 - Honest Labour

Let him that stole steal no more: but rather let him labour, working with his hands the thing which is good, that he may have to give to him that needeth.

There is no implication that the Christians were continuing in a life of crime. Paul was emphasising the change that should be evident from their pre-conversion days when some of them would have been accustomed to pilfering and thieving. An honest day's labour should be their goal so that they would be able to show kindness and help those that were particularly needy. There is no mention here of their own legitimate personal needs although the Scriptures do teach that one should provide for one's own household (1 Thess 4.11; 1 Tim 5.8).

Kindness and mutual support had marked the Church from its first days. In Jerusalem "all that believed were together, and had all things common; And sold their possessions and goods, and parted them to all men, as every man had need" (Acts 2.44-45). In later history, those who shared their property freely with others in a 'community of goods' were castigated as being those who were overthrowing the order in society. 'Mine and thine' were meant to be clearly demarcated and kept that way. In 1527 a brave man called Felix Manz was put to death by being drowned in the Limmat River in Zurich. One of his many 'faults' according to the authorities was his belief that 'a good Christian shares with his neighbour when the latter is in need'.

The Scriptures bring before us the sin of theft in all its shamefulness. It is motivated by covetousness, a lust for something that belongs to another. When the nation of Israel entered Canaan and began their conquest, a crisis arose after their defeat at Ai. Achan's sin in taking and hiding a cache of riches he discovered in Jericho had brought about the tragedy. No progress could be made until his sin was judged (Josh 7.12).

It says much for the Lord Jesus who tolerated in the midst of His band of disciples one called Judas Iscariot. His fatal flaw was a love of money and it is said of Judas, "he was a thief, and had the bag" (Jn 12.6). The

Lord still loved him and gave him time to repent, but he betrayed his Master for a mere handful of silver.

May we be thankful for what the Lord has given to us,
and be generous with it.

4.29 - Edifying Speech

Let no corrupt communication proceed out of your mouth, but that which is good to the use of edifying, that it may minister grace unto the hearers.

The next few verses focus on speech. The contrasts continue between what may have marked the Ephesians' old way of life and what would be expected of their new life in Christ.

The tongue is a powerful little member of the body and it has great potential for good or evil. James wrote that it could be used both to bless God and curse men: "Out of the same mouth proceedeth blessing and cursing. My brethren, these things ought not so to be" (Jas 3.10). To those who might have been used to swearing and blaspheming, the injunction above would have been searching. Had they renounced all such speech?

Conversation among Christians should be upbuilding. Sadly, an evening of what should have been enjoyable and profitable fellowship can quickly be spoiled by the introduction of critical remarks, usually about other believers. The tone quickly degenerates. Some participants come to life and eagerly add their own titbit of gossip. Soon it is apparent that the assembled company has assumed the role of both judge and jury on the life and testimony of another poor victim who has been tried and condemned in their absence. Another character assassination has taken place and a foul smell lingers, for that is what the word 'corrupt' means. It is just a pity that the fragrance of Christ was absent.

Godly hosts and hostesses are wise to all of these pitfalls and will deftly but firmly change the subject to more profitable matters. There are so many things that can encourage us together in conversation: the goodness and mercy of God, blessing in salvation, grace given in a time of trial, a precious thought from the Scriptures, the example of another's life, the growth of a work of God ... The list is endless! When our hearts are in tune with the Master we will find that such times together are too short. We go away rejoicing, strengthened and built up by the sweet and wholesome fellowship of saints. We have had a foretaste of heaven upon earth.

"Let your speech be alway with grace, seasoned with salt." (Col 4.6)

4.30 - Grieving the Holy Spirit

**And grieve not the holy Spirit of God
whereby ye are sealed unto the day of redemption.**

The Holy Spirit of God is grieved when Christians are careless and cruel in their speech. He, our Comforter and Guide, has been ignored, God's Word has been broken, and God's Son has been dishonoured.

The Holy Spirit is one of the triune Godhead. Together the Father, Son, and Holy Spirit are interested in our spiritual welfare. They work in harmony to encourage us and provide all that we need so that we make spiritual progress. The fact that the Spirit indwells the children of God permanently is reassuring; help is always near. But when the prompting of the Spirit is not heeded, He is pained with sorrow. He knows that our thoughtlessness and carelessness will reap a bitter harvest.

Sensitivity to His voice is learned. It proceeds slowly, step by step, when we pause and consider before we say or do anything that might harm others. When He guides, He does so always in accordance with the

Word of God, and always for the glory of the Son of God. The Lord Jesus taught that the Spirit does not speak of Himself but draws attention to the Son. Christ said, "He shall glorify me: for he shall receive of mine, and shall shew it unto you" (Jn 16.14).

The seal of the Spirit has already been referred to (Eph 1.13), and for God's children, it denotes their divine ownership. The seal is secure and can never be 'broken', just as the new birth through the Spirit can never be reversed. In this verse, the duration of the sealing is combined with the thought of its ultimate purpose. The "day of redemption" will take place when Christ returns to the air for His Church. The dead in Christ shall be raised first and the living saints will be transformed. Together they shall be caught up to meet the Lord in the air (1 Thess 4.16-17). Redeemed souls will be united with glorified bodies. Never again will our bodies be subject to decay and corruption, and never again will the flesh have any influence over us. The fulness of redemption will be manifested in that the saints will, at last, be like their glorious Lord. We look expectantly for that coming day (Phil 3.20-21).

The Spirit of God is holy and He wants us to be holy also.

4.31 - Bitterness

Let all bitterness, and wrath, and anger, and clamour, and evil speaking, be put away from you, with all malice:

Here is a group of negative and destructive evils that are rooted in bitterness and anger. They are manifested in speech. They all threaten the unity and welfare of God's people and can ruin a Christian testimony overnight.

Medical science recognises a growing number of serious conditions which are labelled as 'autoimmune'. These include rheumatoid arthritis, type 1 diabetes, coeliac disease, and multiple sclerosis. These debilitating diseases are often difficult to treat. The underlying problem is that the body attacks its own cells and begins to destroy itself.

This underscores the fact that a body will suffer if it is attacking itself. In the context of local church life, constant internal warfare may tear an assembly apart. Paul faced up to the reality of these dangers and forthrightly commanded the Ephesians to avoid all such behaviour. (Notice the repetition of the word 'all' at the beginning and end of the sentence.) Elsewhere Paul gave another pertinent warning: "But if ye bite and devour one another, take heed that ye be not consumed one of another" (Gal 5.15).

Bitterness of heart stems from frustration, often fuelled by envy or jealousy: a person does not get their own way, fails to achieve their goals, or feels slighted when they are not given the place or recognition they think they deserve. The response to these frustrations is acidic and poisonous.

The mental turmoil generated by a bitter spirit usually becomes focused on others. The victims can suffer a hostile onslaught of harsh words and slanderous accusations, and be left deeply wounded. These wounds may heal but slowly and leave persistent painful scars.

The world in which we live has become increasingly fractious and divided. Political turmoil on every continent has resulted in strife, wars and immense suffering. Vociferous protest movements try to shout down their rivals. The trading of insults through the media is commonplace. And yet it is in the morass of this world that the Church is to continue bearing a clear testimony to the Lord. A boat in a turbulent sea is one thing; the sea coming into the boat is quite another. Only by God's grace can we be preserved from allowing the world and its ways to flood the Church.

Let us not do the devil's work for him.

4.32 - Forgiveness

And be ye kind one to another, tenderhearted, forgiving one another, even as God for Christ's sake hath forgiven you.

It is with relief that we leave behind the oppressive smog of the valley and recommence our climb. We break out into the fresh, clean air of the mountainside and joyfully breathe our fill. The contrasts could not be greater: from the hardness, harshness and ugliness of this world to the kindness, tenderness and loveliness that should mark the followers of Christ.

This verse and the two related verses that follow were not afterthoughts with Paul. (The chapter division is not in the best place.) He leads us to higher ground, the heights of grace.

Kindness is an attitude of mind and heart that looks outwards to others, and seeks to bless and help them in practical ways. It is also infectious, affecting others. We are exhorted to become kind, and then go on being kind. This is not a piece of optional advice but an authoritative command.

To be tenderhearted translates a word that originally describes one's innermost being. It has the idea of being deeply moved from within and conveys the idea of pity and compassion.

If our hearts are kind and tenderhearted, it will not be difficult to forgive others. Paul links this with our own forgiveness. How have we been forgiven? The standard is high, for God has forgiven us freely and fully in Christ. He has not done so at the expense of His holiness or righteousness; God never overlooks sin nor should we. But what God did was to send His spotless Son to pay for our sins at Calvary. The Scriptures declare that without the shedding of blood there can be no remission (Heb 9.22). Through the finished work of Christ upon the cross, God remains just and yet can be the justifier of those who believe in Jesus (Rom 3.26).

Paul suffered much injustice in his life and yet it did not leave him embittered. He could recall the great evil that was done to him by Alexander the coppersmith – he gave no details – and then there were disappointments when Demas, and others too, forsook him (2 Tim 4.10, 14, 16). He remained thankful, joyful and hopeful right to the end, because he had a forgiving spirit and practised what he preached. He would have agreed that an unforgiving Christian is a contradiction in terms.

Those who have been so freely forgiven should be forgiving.

Chapter 5

Shine Brighter

*Paul exhorts the Christians to continue walking lovingly, purely,
and wisely.
They are to shine as lights in the darkness of this world.
Their marriages should be marked by love and submission,
as a fitting picture of the relationship between Christ
and the Church.*

5.1-21   HOLY TESTIMONY
5.22-33 HOLY MATRIMONY

5.1 - Likeness

Be ye therefore followers of God, as dear children;

Paul's words of appeal stem from his warm affection for these believers. He is further encouraging them to display godliness in the way they treat one another.

Apart from the words of Scripture in which God has revealed His character, the world might have had reason to complain that there was never any visible example of what true godliness looked like. Men who portrayed some aspect of God's character were marred by other personal weaknesses. Indeed, the greatest of men failed on their strongest points: Abraham, the great man of faith, on several occasions panicked in fear; Moses, the meekest man upon the earth, was once disobedient through anger; David had some of the highest thoughts but committed some of the lowest deeds; Samson demonstrated physical strength but was morally weak; and Solomon was so wise at the beginning but ended up so foolish. With the coming into the world of the Lord Jesus Christ all this changed. The fulness of Deity became visible in perfect humanity, and for over thirty-three years He lived among men. He could say, "He that hath seen me hath seen the Father" (Jn 14.9). He had no strong points because He had no weak ones.

To follow God is synonymous with following Christ and seeking to be more like Him. It is not merely a superficial and temporary imitation that is in view, but a deep lasting transformation of character. This occurs as we spend time in fellowship with Him. As we gaze upon Him, slowly but surely we are "changed into the same image from glory to glory, even as by the Spirit of the Lord" (2 Cor 3.18).

The apostle Paul was always clear that the example of his life was only valid in the measure in which he emulated Christ: "Be ye followers of me, even as I also am of Christ" (1 Cor 11.1). On another occasion, he related how the Thessalonian Christians had followed his example. They, in turn, became a shining example to others in the whole region:

"And ye became followers of us, and of the Lord, having received the word in much affliction, with joy of the Holy Ghost: So that ye were ensamples to all that believe in Macedonia and Achaia" (1 Thess 1.6-7). This was how it was meant to be. The torch of testimony is passed on in this way.

In the context of our verse, Paul is still considering the matter of kindness, and there is none so kind as God. He gives to us so that we can give to others.

True godliness is seen in Christ.

5.2 - Fragrance

And walk in love, as Christ also hath loved us, and hath given himself for us an offering and a sacrifice to God for a sweetsmelling savour.

The supreme example of Christ is lifted up to show clearly the essence of divine love – sacrificial giving for others. The phrase "as Christ" will reappear later in this chapter in the context of marriage (Eph 5.23, 25).

If believers are to be marked by kindness, tenderness, and forgiveness in their relationships with one another, these can only be maintained by the wellspring of love. Divine love is a love that gives. It is an action, not an emotion. There are two notable aspects to the death of Christ: it was a sacrifice offered to God, and it was a sacrifice given for us. Other scriptures affirm the breadth of this truth: Christ "through the eternal Spirit offered himself without spot to God" (Heb 9.14); He Himself could say "I am the good shepherd: the good shepherd giveth his life for the sheep" (Jn 10.11). When Christ gave His life, He gave His all. Nothing was held back; it was completely poured out (Is 53.12).

Sacrificial giving brings pleasure to the heart of God and blessing to others. A fragrance ascends heavenward as a sweet savour, just like that which arose from the burnt offering in the tabernacle (Lev 1.13). All of the levitical offerings pointed forward to the death of Christ. Paul spoke joyfully of a gift from the Philippians, describing it as "an odour of a sweet smell, a sacrifice acceptable, wellpleasing to God" (Phil 4.18). God was honoured and Paul was blessed.

This principle is revolutionary. Any act of sacrificial love and kindness shown to others, no matter how small or insignificant it might seem, can become an act of worship. If it is done for Christ's sake, a fragrance ascends heavenwards. In fact, everything can be done for His glory as well as the blessing of others. "And whatsoever ye do in word or deed, do all in the name of the Lord Jesus, giving thanks to God and the Father by Him"; "And whatsoever ye do, do it heartily, as to the Lord, and not unto men" (Col 3.17, 23). When this principle is applied, there is no division of life into the sacred, for God, and the secular for ourselves. He is worthy of all we are and have (Rom 12.1).

Why should we not live every moment of the day for His glory?

5.3 - Purity

But fornication, and all uncleanness, or covetousness, let it not be once named among you, as becometh saints;

Common topics of worldly conversation – acts of sexual immorality, salacious gossip, and illicit relationships – are never to be discussed among believers. They are not fitting matters for saints to dwell upon. Covetousness here is a wide term and includes a lustful desire for someone else's body (Ex 20.17).

The world is awash with sights and sounds that are attractive to the flesh. The billion-dollar entertainment, media, and advertising industries are well aware of the selling potential of such imagery and lyrics. The constant bombardment has the effect of dulling the mind, so that one can unconsciously begin to accept these things as normal, or at least regard them as being not particularly harmful.

There will be challenges for parents in the home, particularly regarding supervision. Children are generally more adept at using technology than their parents. They routinely converse, or sometimes whisper, about things that the parents have never heard of – 'apps', games, films and songs that are currently 'trending'. The father and mother will be wise to have some understanding of these pressures. Together they should agree to define clear boundaries that establish their home as a place where Christ is honoured.

The school environment also moulds the minds of the children in attendance. Some schools retain a Christian ethos while others are decidedly biased against any religious influence. The liberal mindset and values of teaching staff are easily imbibed by impressionable young people.

The workplace is fraught with challenges. One only has to read the story of the young boy, Samuel, left by his mother to serve in the temple, to wonder how he could ever manage to remain uncorrupted. The sons of Eli were self-willed and shamelessly immoral, and they could so easily have trained the lad in their ways. Surely, the power of a mother's prayers came into the equation (1 Sam 1.27). Hannah had been a praying woman before Samuel was born, and without doubt, she continued to be the same after she had fulfilled her vow and given him back to the Lord. By the grace of God, the young man's life was preserved, and he grew up to be a force for good in the nation of Israel.

There will be occasions in assembly life when elders are obliged to discuss unpleasant and painful matters, if sin has come to light among those under their care. They will do so privately, confidentially, and prayerfully.

Before God, purity is the pathway to power.

5.4 - Thankfulness

**Neither filthiness, nor foolish talking, nor jesting,
which are not convenient: but rather giving of thanks.**

Paul concludes his exhortations about the kind of speech that should mark the believer and that which should be completely rejected. He leaves us in no doubt that smutty and suggestive talk is prohibited. The entertainment industry relies heavily on off-colour jokes to generate laughs. There is hardly such a thing today as a 'clean' comedian.

Is there any place in life for humour? Some people of a serious disposition feel that it also is unbecoming, and the Bible does not give any licence for it. However, others have found that gentle humour or laughter, often at one's own expense, has relieved the tension of an otherwise perplexing situation. The lady of the house cannot find her spectacles. She begins a frantic search all around her home, under cushions, in cupboards, and elsewhere. She is growing increasingly frustrated until she happens to glance in the mirror, only to find that her spectacles are safely perched on her nose! She bursts out in laughter at her own foolishness. She might well tell her husband when he comes home and he will probably be amused as well. Most of us can relate to this. But to be always joking and laughing in a flippant manner, particularly about the mistakes or misfortunes of others, would be both unwise and unkind. Certainly, in the main, life should not be regarded as 'a laughing matter' at all when there are such serious and eternal issues at stake.

Paul does not leave matters in a vacuum; he extols the habit of giving thanks. There are those who will never mention anything off-colour in their speech but who constantly complain and criticise. They too are wide off the mark.

The Christian has a myriad of reasons to be thankful every day. The praising Christian is neither a blind optimist nor a deluded escapist; he is a joyful realist. He knows for sure that he is loved with an everlasting loved, he has been forgiven of every sin, and he is on his way to a glorious and eternal home. To these can be added many other reasons why he can go through the day joyfully and thankfully. It all depends on our point of view: looking within we feel discouraged; looking around we feel depressed; but when we look above, we are delighted. Our Saviour awaits us there.

Leave the complaining to others; let us travel home praising.

5.5 – The Kingdom

For this ye know, that no whoremonger, nor unclean person, nor covetous man, who is an idolater, hath any inheritance in the kingdom of Christ and of God.

The stark truth contained in this verse is categoric and solemn; it is the conclusion of that which has gone before. Paul explains that the Ephesians should know already that those whose lives are characterised by these sinful patterns of behaviour have no part in God's kingdom (mentioned only here in Ephesians).

All immoral habits and attitudes are included in this statement, particularly in the realm of sexual behaviour. Covetousness and idolatry are both linked again with an unclean and dissolute lifestyle. The lust for that which is physical and that which is not one's own means that God is forgotten. An idol is anything that is put before God: in the relentless pursuit of pleasure, men and women are rejecting God's rule in their lives and instead enthroning self and the flesh. Their passions rule and control their lives. Romans 1 sums this up, describing how mankind turned away from God "and changed the glory of the uncorruptible God into an image made like to corruptible man ... Wherefore God also gave them up to uncleanness through the lusts of their own hearts, to dishonour their own bodies between themselves: Who changed the truth of God into a lie, and worshipped and served the creature more than the Creator" (Rom 1.23-25).

The kingdom of Christ and of God is one kingdom. It may be that the present form of the kingdom is associated more with the Lord Jesus who came to proclaim that kingdom upon earth. He announced the holy standards of that kingdom, exceeding the Mosaic law: "Ye have heard that is was said by them of old time, Thou shalt not commit adultery: But I say unto you, That whosoever looketh on a woman to lust after her hath committed adultery with her already in his heart" (Mt 5.27-28).

The King was rejected by His people but His kingdom programme continues in this present Church age. It is not yet established in a visible form. This will change when Christ returns to earth in power and glory and sets up His millennial kingdom. Finally, this kingdom will be handed over to the Father: "Then cometh the end, when he shall have delivered up the kingdom to God, even the Father" (1 Cor 15.24).

The King is coming!

5.6 - The Truth

Let no man deceive you with vain words: for because of these things cometh the wrath of God upon the children of disobedience.

Paul was aware that a continual barrage of arguments might be presented to the believers, denying the seriousness of a sinful lifestyle: 'Everyone is doing it'; 'That is just how we are'; 'There are much worse things, like murder'; 'A loving God understands'. No matter from whatever quarter such words might come, from unbelieving people of the world or even from professing Christians, the Ephesians were to know that these words were false and dangerous.

Imagine someone who deliberately removes warning signs from the motorway, with the excuse that they want to make the driving experience more pleasant and enjoyable, and not cause anyone any anxiety. The actual outcome would be to make the driving experience a road to death, causing multiple fatal accidents. In the Word of God, warnings are always issued in love – they are not threats issued in malice – so that people might heed them and avoid the pain, shame, and disaster that follows if they are not heeded.

God holds people responsible for their actions and their lifestyles. There is within the heart of every man a conscience which signals that an act is right or wrong. Even those who have never read the Scriptures are aware that stealing is a violation.

The wrath of God stems from His fixed disposition against all evil. God's response in judging it will be shown to be righteous in every respect. It will be individual in that each unbelieving person will stand before His great white throne. There will be no verdict given unjustly or in absentia. It will be proportionate in that every individual sinner will be judged according to his or her own works. The books hold a record of every transgression (Rev 20.12). The evidence will be clear and plain to all.

Some think that they might have 'got away with it' and their misdeeds will be forgotten about. "Because sentence against an evil work is not executed speedily, therefore the heart of the sons of men is fully set in them to do evil" (Eccl 8:11). They might claim defiantly that there is no God, no afterlife, and no eternal punishment. They will persist in repeating these bold assertions with their lips, even when their consciences are telling them otherwise.

God is holy and righteous and nothing misses His gaze.

5. 7 - Separation

Be not ye therefore partakers with them.

This is both a conclusion and an instruction to stay away from those who commit evil. Believers are to maintain a clear line of separation, so that they do not join together either with those who practise a sinful lifestyle or with those who would seek to condone it.

The important issue of separation from sin needs to be clarified. Firstly, it should stem for a deep desire to do everything we can to please the Lord. It goes together with an equal determination to do nothing that would displease Him. The positive and negative aspects are complementary. Love for Christ is at the heart of it.

Secondly, separation does not mean isolation from others or withdrawing from society. While God's servants have at times been called to be alone with Him, they have all been sent back "into the world" to serve Him (Jn 17.18). There is no warrant for living as a hermit in a cave or as a monk behind the wall of a monastery. Christian testimony is only effective if it is "in the world" (Jn 17.11), and is motivated by love for sinners.

Thirdly, Christian testimony is only effective if it is "not of the world" (Jn 17.14, 16). Separation from sin contrasts with the worldview and lifestyle of unbelievers and is unavoidably confrontational. It is this difference that the Holy Spirit uses to bring conviction. Some Christians go to great lengths to blend in and not stick out. They do not want to appear to be judgmental or make others feel uncomfortable. The problem is that unbelievers may feel nothing at all, and may not be convicted in this way if there is no obvious difference: 'Why would I ever want to be like you if you are just the same as me?'

Fourthly, separation from sin should be a personal exercise clothed in humility. When Christians look down upon unbelievers they forget what they once were themselves. The Israelites were prone to make this mistake and despise or mistreat the strangers (foreigners) in their midst. They seemed to have had conveniently short memories. They had to be reminded and cautioned, "Thou shalt not vex a stranger, nor oppress him: for ye were strangers in the land of Egypt" (Ex 22.21). It does us good to remember what we once were so that we will not be affected by pride. Love, humility, and kindness are always to mark God's people.

This world is not our home; we belong to another land.

5. 8 - Children of Light

For ye were sometimes darkness, but now are ye light in the Lord: walk as children of light:

The apostle did not say that the believers were once in the darkness, although that would have been equally true of their position as sinners, but that they had been darkness. In other words, the darkness was in them. Since their conversion, the light was now in them. The Lord Jesus Christ had declared "I am the light of the world: he that followeth me shall not walk in darkness, but shall have the light of life" (Jn 8.12). The Ephesian believers had received Christ as Saviour and were indwelt by His own Spirit of light and truth. They were being exhorted to continue being a bright testimony to others who were still in darkness.

Those afflicted with the eye disease, glaucoma, may develop a complication known as a scotoma (from the same word used in this verse for 'darkness'). With increased pressure inside the eye, the optic nerve fibres can degenerate causing irreversible damage and eventual blindness. Sadly, when this occurs, there is no cure. Thank God, sinners who were once darkness can become light.

Contrasting light and darkness is a figurative way of considering the age-old moral battle between good and evil. The devil has always been trying to obliterate every glimmer of truth and hope in the world. His mission is to blind the minds and hearts of men and women. His final destination is darkness, and he is seeking to take others with him: "the god of this world hath blinded the minds of them which believe not, lest the light of the glorious gospel of Christ, who is the image of God, should shine unto them" (2 Cor 4.4).

When God and His Word are resisted or rejected there is only moral darkness. Men love darkness rather than light because their deeds are evil, declared the apostle John (Jn 3.19). They avoid the light, knowing that it will expose their sin. Furthermore, when men choose darkness over light, their perception becomes defective and their darkness only increases (Mt 6.23). God, by His sovereign will, may also send darkness as a manifestation of His judgment upon sin and evil, but when men fail to repent they sink even lower; they become more like the brute beasts of the field than those created in the image of God (Rom 1.21-28). Moral darkness conceals the pathway of truth and destroys the ability to distinguish right from wrong.

Love the light and be the light.

5.9 - Fruit

(For the fruit of the Spirit is in all goodness and righteousness and truth;)

The effects of being light in the Lord will become evident. In the physical world it only takes a small light to overcome intense darkness. One can walk into a completely dark room and ignite a match; immediately the darkness is dispelled and that which was 'hidden' becomes visible.

In a dark and evil world, the shining testimony of a believer can radiate goodness. This general term covers morality in its many aspects. Significantly, the word used for goodness is only found in the Bible and does not occur in other Greek texts of that time. It denotes active goodness that looks out for the welfare of others and moves to assist them. In the beginning, all that God created was "very good" (Gen 1.31), but through the work of the devil and the entrance of sin, creation was marred. The heart of man was robbed of its innocence. God's command was disobeyed and men thought only of pleasing themselves.

Righteousness, as seen in God's children, is a reflection of the just and holy character of God. It is the undeviating commitment to act morally, in a way that is pleasing to God and is according to His Word. One's relationship to God and to others is properly maintained by reverence for the Lord and respect for one's neighbour. It is so often an absent quality in the world today. Individuals and governments manoeuvre and often cheat to give themselves an advantage.

Truth has already been mentioned by Paul when he encouraged the believers to speak the truth in love and to put away lying (Eph 4.15, 25). How we speak is only one aspect of truth. How we think and act are also integral parts of a Christian's testimony. Where can truth be found? It is the Word of God that declares it and the Son of God who embodies it. All of our thoughts, words, and deeds, should be according to these unchanging realities. In the world at large, 'truth' is an elastic concept that can change to suit the prevailing conditions. Two sides relate two different stories, each claiming to tell the truth. Often both parties have bent it.

To be good, right, and true may not be regarded as the most sought after virtues in society but they have always been important before God.

Our spiritual fruit is evidence of the light within.

5.10 - Pleasing Him

Proving what is acceptable unto the Lord.

There is always a choice involved in daily living. We might live to please only ourselves, putting self first every time. This would amount to idolatry. We might aim to please others and make a good impression on them. This would make us slaves to public opinion and only men-pleasers (Col 3.22). Paul here is upholding the gold standard for our lives as Christians: to live in a way that is acceptable and pleasing to the Lord according to the light He has given. He should be at the centre of our lives, and His opinion is the only one that matters.

In the life of Christ, we have the perfect example. He said of His Father, "I do always those things that please him" (Jn 8.29), and again "I came down from heaven, not to do mine own will, but the will of him that sent me" (Jn 6.38). In His hour of deepest woe He prayed, "Not my will, but thine, be done" (Lk 22.42).

Paul's life was also focused on pleasing the Lord who had chosen him to be a soldier (2 Tim 2.4). That is why he purposely did not entangle himself with worldly matters that had little eternal significance. He urged others to present their bodies as "a living sacrifice, holy, acceptable unto God"; this he described as their reasonable service (Rom 12.1). On account of all that God had done for them in His mercy, this was the only fitting response.

It is still routine practice for precious metals – gold and silver – to be tested as to their quality. When they are found to be pure, they are approved. When they are not pure, they fail the test and are disapproved. The same idea is implied here in the approval or disapproval of our testimony by the Lord. There is a present aspect in seeking to please the Lord now, but there is also a future examination that lies ahead. All service will be examined before the judgment seat of Christ by the Lord Himself. An individual's service will receive its commensurate reward according to its quality (1 Cor 3.12-14). Perhaps the best reward will be to hear our Lord say, "Well done, thou good and faithful servant" (Mt 25.21).

May we always seek to please the Lord.

5.11 - No Fellowship

And have no fellowship with the unfruitful works of darkness, but rather reprove them.

This is a clear prohibition against fellowship with evil deeds and those who practise them. The believer is not to participate in them. It may have been the case in Ephesus that there were believers who had remained in some kind of partnership with unbelievers; this was a command to stop.

Writing to the Corinthians who had many such problems of retaining habits from their old life, Paul had said, "Be ye not unequally yoked together with unbelievers: for what fellowship hath righteousness with unrighteousness? and what communion hath light with darkness? And what concord hath Christ with Belial? or what part hath he that believeth with an infidel? And what agreement hath the temple of God with idols? for ye are the temple of the living God; as God hath said, I will dwell in them, and walk in them; and I will be their God, and they shall be my people. Wherefore come out from among them, and be ye separate, saith the Lord, and touch not the unclean thing; and I will receive you" (2 Cor 6.14-17). This was an unequivocal call to come apart and stay apart. Only by separation could one retain integrity as a child of God, thereby maintaining holiness and exposing sinfulness.

Being unequally yoked together applies to a marriage in which a believer has married an unbeliever, swayed by their affections and desire to have a partner for life. It applies to a business partnership in which a believer may have been won over by the apparent guarantee of financial success. Such 'fellowships' can seem attractive, and many reasons are cited why they are 'working': 'Look how happy we are together', or 'We have made such a tidy profit, and given quite a bit to charity as well'. God declares such ventures to be unfruitful.

Those who are in such relationships are often prickly if anyone suggests that they are acting in disobedience to the Word of God. The question must remain: "What communion hath light with darkness?" (2 Cor 6.14). Compromising the truth and tolerating darkness is folly. On a practical level, while the light and its influence may not be extinguished entirely, it is always dimmed and therefore easily overcome.

"God is light, and in him is no darkness at all." (1 Jn 1.5)

5.12 - Shame

**For it is a shame even to speak of those things which are done
of them in secret.**

Paul must have been offended at times to hear believers speaking openly
of sinful things. In this letter he had already warned against corrupt
speech (Eph 4.29), and conversation that dwelt on sexual immorality
(Eph 5.3). Here he counselled and warned against conversing about
things done in secret. These things would have included immoral acts,
as already mentioned, but also forms of magic and occult practices.

While it is necessary to confront, rebuke, and warn about evil deeds,
the words used should be carefully considered beforehand. Mature,
godly men will use plain and unambiguous language while at the same
time being sensitive to their audience. There may be young children
present, or older people unused to public references to these kinds of
sin. Generally speaking, excessive details are unnecessary. In matters of
assembly discipline, it is often necessary to counsel the saints that the
matters disclosed are not for open discussion in homes or elsewhere
outside the assembly.

The apostle was aware of the depressing and harmful effect of dwelling
upon evil and going into the lurid details. The mind is so impressionable
that it is rarely left unscathed. Reports in recent years have related that
police officers trained to uncover criminal activities were so shocked
and traumatised by evidence they uncovered, that afterwards they
required professional counselling.

The verse teaches that the things done in secret were so sordid that even
those who perpetrated them attempted to keep them hidden. "And this
is the condemnation, that light is come into the world, and men loved
darkness rather than light, because their deeds were evil. For every
one that doeth evil hateth the light, neither cometh to the light, lest his
deeds should be reproved" (Jn 3.19-20).

In the African context, the prevalence of witchcraft is also evidence of the continued power of darkness. It is not uncommon for even rich and educated people to be dominated by fear and suspicion. If they are successful, they begin to fear that others will be jealous and try to bewitch them. If things are not going so well, they fear that they have already been bewitched. Whatever the case, they will consult a traditional doctor. At times dark and evil deeds have been perpetrated to acquire medicine strong enough to give adequate protection.

May we talk in the light as well as walk in the light.

5.13 - Reproval

But all things that are reproved are made manifest by the light: for whatsoever doth make manifest is light.

The light exposes the things that were hidden in the darkness. The Word of God, when brought to bear upon evil, shows up sin for what it really is, and condemns it outright. Sin is rooted in independent self-will and rebellion against God.

King David, when he sinned and committed adultery with the wife of Uriah, devised an elaborate plan to cover up his transgression. It is painful to observe not only the intricate web of deception but also the sheer cruelty involved when ultimately the brave and faithful soldier was sent to his certain death. How treacherous it was to arrange to have Uriah placed in the forefront of the battle and then issue a secret command for all the rest of his comrades to suddenly withdraw and leave him exposed and alone – the ultimate betrayal.

When David heard the report of the battle and Uriah's death, he thought that the matter had been sufficiently covered up. It might have been, had not God seen it all: "But the thing that David had done displeased the Lord" (2 Sam 11.27). Through Nathan, the prophet, the vile and pitiless sin was exposed. David was never quite the same again and his family and the nation would continue to suffer the consequences. God said to him, "For thou didst it secretly: but I will do this thing before all Israel, and before the sun" (2 Sam 12.12). The light had revealed all.

If light both convicts and condemns sin, there is also a more positive side to it. As in David's case, it can bring repentance and change. Those who have responded to God's convicting light and allowed it to transform them, will themselves become a source of light to others. Light spreads light. One candle ignites another. This is probably what Paul had in mind when he thought of the Ephesians and their conversion to God. They had come out from darkness and now could be light to others.

When the Lord Jesus was upon earth, His enemies soon were planning His death. What must have shocked and troubled them was that the Lord knew what they were thinking. Their secrets were not secrets to Him: "And Jesus knowing their thoughts said, Wherefore think ye evil in your hearts?" (Mt 9.4).

So live that even your private moments can stand the Lord's inspection.

5.14 - Awake!

Wherefore he saith, Awake thou that sleepest, and arise from the dead, and Christ shall give thee light.

Here is a call to action. It cannot be traced directly to any known passage elsewhere in the Scriptures (Is 60.1-2 has a slight similarity), and so it is difficult to be precise about the identity of "he", or even the definition of "it" if the alternative translation is preferred.

The call is framed as a gospel appeal to those asleep and dead in their sins. The darkness in their case is not just that of the sin itself but of being careless about their state. The three short clauses may have been part of one of the first 'gospel hymns'.

Those who are asleep in their sins are unconcerned about their spiritual condition before God and their eternal destiny. In Acts 16 the keeper of the prison in Philippi was both physically and spiritually asleep. It took a great earthquake to rouse him from that sleep and to cause him concern about the matter of his soul's salvation. It was a night of miracles in that no one was injured or killed, no prisoner escaped, and best of all, the jailer was converted after one of the shortest gospel messages was proclaimed: "Believe on the Lord Jesus Christ, and thou shalt be saved" (Acts 16.31). Those who preach the gospel have a solemn duty to make the life-giving message clear and plain, but divine power is needed, the power of the Holy Spirit, to bring conviction of sin and enlightenment to blinded minds and hearts.

The deadness of sinners has already been described in an earlier chapter of the letter (Eph 2.1). This speaks of the absence of eternal life and the inability to do anything to save oneself. However, there remains the ability, indeed the responsibility, to answer the gospel call. No sinner is able to raise himself from the deadness of sin, but he does have the ability to trust in the One who has the power to do so, the Lord Jesus Christ, who conquered death and arose from among the dead.

At the tomb of Lazarus, Christ issued three authoritative commands: "Take ye away the stone" and let in the light; "Lazarus, come forth" and partake of life; "Loose him, and let him go" and enjoy liberty (Jn 11.39, 43, 44). With joyful wonder Lazarus came forth!

Christ alone is the light of life.

5.15 - Wisdom

See then that ye walk circumspectly, not as fools, but as wise,

Having emphasised the darkness and evil in the world, Paul also introduced a note of urgency, especially for those who were spiritually asleep. This prompted him to exhort the Christians to be careful as to how they should live in the midst of such an environment. There were many 'potholes' on the pathway of life and he desired that the saints should avoid them.

The wise believer will look carefully at his manner of life and assess it critically before the Lord. There is nothing to be commended in thoughtlessly and carelessly drifting through life with the attitude, 'I am what I am'. The vital question is, 'Am I what I should be?' Each life has eternal significance: it can be lived for God's glory and the blessing of others, or it can be squandered by self-indulgence and laziness. The choice and contrast could not be starker – will I be wise or foolish?

There are two kinds of wisdom according to the Scriptures. At the beginning of his letter to the Corinthians, Paul contrasted the wisdom of God with the wisdom of this world. The two are complete opposites. One is spiritual and the other is natural. The apostle understood that when the gospel of the crucified Christ was proclaimed, some regarded it as foolishness: "But we preach Christ crucified, unto the Jews a stumblingblock, and unto the Greeks foolishness" (1 Cor 1.23). The Jews had refused to believe that Jesus was the Messiah – how could the true Messiah end up on a shameful cross? The Gentile Greeks had a different perspective. They pursued the philosophies of men as a means of self-advancement, and so the concept of a humble carpenter ending His life in defeat had little appeal for them either.

Worldly wisdom is still in conflict with the Word of God. The world says, 'Live as you like and do what you like. Have a good time, as long as nobody is harmed. Don't worry about tomorrow.' Paul was teaching that Christians are to live to be obedient and pleasing before the Lord. Holiness matters. Love and kindness matter. We are not here for ourselves; we are here to serve God, to serve our fellow brothers and sisters in Christ, and to be a clear and faithful testimony to a perishing world. We should have an eye on eternity.

Godly wisdom is often regarded as foolishness by the world.

5.16 - Time

Redeeming the time, because the days are evil.

Our view of time and how we manage it says much about our core beliefs. All of us have the same number of minutes in the day. Some people are remarkably productive and seem to accomplish a lot using those minutes, whereas others fritter away half the day in matters of little consequence.

Paul was urging the believers to buy up every moment in the sense of grasping every opportunity to serve and glorify God. At least three reasons might be considered for his exhortation:

Firstly, the evil days and the deepening darkness meant that the need for the light to shine was even greater. If the days were evil in Paul's time in the first century, how much more today? Take a glance at any national newspaper and the headlines are a continual stream of bad news with trouble and strife all over the world. Disorder and chaos, violence and rebellion, as well as an open disregard for God and His Word, are the order of the day.

Secondly, time is short in view of the Lord's return for His Church. Paul expressed a hope that he might still be alive when the Lord returned for the saints: "Then we which are alive and remain shall be caught up together with them [resurrected saints] in the clouds, to meet the Lord in the air" (1 Thess 4.17). If Paul felt that the Lord's return was imminent, how much more should we be living in the expectation that He could come soon? No signs need to be fulfilled before He comes to the air and calls His people home. All opportunities for service will then be over. For the unbelieving, the day of grace will have ended and the door of salvation will have closed.

Thirdly, the certainty of divine judgment upon an ungodly world should be an urgent incentive to rescue the lost. There lies ahead a final judgment that no unbeliever will escape. It is described as "a great white throne" upon which a holy God sits in awesome power and glory. Every unbeliever will stand before that throne, the books will be opened, no sin will be overlooked, and the judgment will be eternal (Rev 20.11-15).

Seize today, and make it count for the Lord.

5.17 – The Lord's Will

Wherefore be ye not unwise, but understanding what the will of the Lord is.

To navigate safely through the darkness and evil of this world, and because of the lateness of the hour, the child of God will require wisdom from above. Godly wisdom results in a focused, purposeful life. Being unwise in this verse is not ignorance but an attitude of mind and heart that disregards what is known to be true. Paul was issuing a command to the saints to stop being careless and thoughtless about fulfilling God's will for their lives.

Young Christians particularly are interested in knowing what the will of the Lord is for their lives and they often ask the question, 'How can I know God's will for my life?' They want to know in advance what great plan God has in store for them. While this desire is a healthy one, it reveals a certain misunderstanding.

Knowing the will of God is not like an on-off switch. The questioner above implies that he or she presently does not know the will of God, but awaits some startling revelation that will suddenly make everything clear. Scriptural examples of men like the prophet Elijah are helpful. God directed him to Cherith, then to Zarephath, then on to King Ahab, before he confronted the false prophets on Mount Carmel. God was preparing him and teaching him valuable lessons in each place. His guidance was step by step.

The following advice may be helpful to those who are seeking to know the will of God. (It assumes that one's present location and occupation are not a direct result of disobedience to the voice of God.) Firstly, do what you can for the Lord to the best of your ability, using what gifts He has given you, and where He has placed you for the present. He has you there for a reason. Secondly, maintain your daily communion with Him through reading His Word and praying, so that you hear Him speaking and are sensitive to His voice. Thirdly, continue on this pathway until He sends you somewhere else or asks you to do something else. Finally, be prepared to obey, to move or change as He directs.

There is no mystery to this matter of knowing and carrying out the Lord's will. Day by day, and step by step, we simply seek to honour and obey Him.

On life's pathway the Lord is our closest friend, counsellor and guide.

5.18 - Spirit-Filled

And be not drunk with wine, wherein is excess;
but be filled with the Spirit;

Knowing the will of God and carrying it out is possible for every believer because God has provided all that we need. Hindrances remain and one of the 'potholes' Paul identifies is a love of wine leading to drunkenness. In a state of intoxication, no one thinks straight or acts appropriately. In fact, drunkenness is a sure way to ruin one's testimony and bring disgrace upon the Name of the Lord we profess to love.

Consider the following scenarios, all related to the abuse of alcohol: innocent pedestrians are mown down and killed by an inebriated driver; self-control disappears and acts of immorality and unfaithfulness are committed; people become abusive and violently assault others; money is squandered leaving a family destitute; marriages are split asunder; and body and mind are destroyed. The list of sad consequences arising from drunkenness is endless.

Paul follows his prohibition of drunkenness with a positive command that will make all the difference to our lives. It is not a once-for-all filling but a continuous filling with, or literally 'in', the Holy Spirit. A Spirit-filled Christian has a power and influence for blessing that nothing of this world could ever equal.

Every believer is indwelt by the Holy Spirit from the moment of conversion. As we have learnt from this letter, the Holy Spirit is the seal of ownership and the guarantor of the inheritance to come (Eph 1.13-14). We do not receive part of Him but all of Him; He is a divine Person. The important question must be, 'How much does the Holy Spirit have of us?' In other words, how yielded and responsive are we to Him leading and guiding us through the Word? Are there areas of our lives from which He is still excluded?

Consider how a guest might be received in your home. You make sure that certain rooms have been cleaned and are presentable, but there may be other rooms that you keep locked? They are untidy, maybe even dusty, and you did not get round to sorting them out or cleaning them. You hope that the guest will not want to venture there!

The Holy Spirit wants to have access to all the 'rooms' or departments of our lives and to have full control. He exposes anything that is not right and helps us to correct it so that we can please the Lord. Sin will have to be removed, and love of self will have to go. It is only when we empty ourselves of every hindrance that He can fill us completely.

We cannot be 'full of ourselves' and full of the Spirit
at the same time.

5.19 - Singing

**Speaking to yourselves in psalms and hymns and spiritual
songs, singing and making melody in your heart
to the Lord;**

Being filled with the Spirit is linked here with two beneficial accompaniments; being filled with the Scriptures and being filled with song. These perfectly complement each other.

Speaking to yourselves means to speak to one another about the Scriptures. This implies that the believer is reading the Word of God and meditating upon it by turning it over in the mind and enjoying it in the soul, then the blessing is shared with others. The recommended dose for personal Bible reading is at least once a day but for a prime condition of health, the daily dose can be increased. There is no such thing as an overdose.

Most of us are adept and vocal when we speak to one another about the weather, the cost of living, health problems, or any other such subject of daily life. When it comes to raising the matter of the Scriptures in conversation, we suddenly become embarrassed and tongue-tied. There are those inspirational individuals who have developed the knack of sharing the good things of God in conversation. They are not doing so to display their superior knowledge, or to make one feel inadequate or unspiritual. Their personal and deep-seated joy is simply overflowing.

The Psalms have a special appeal in that they encompass the full range of human emotions and fit all occasions. Past generations have arranged them in a metrical version suitable for singing. "Hymns and spiritual songs" are not easily distinguished. The first may have been a formal or extended setting of Scriptures to music, whereas a spiritual song might have been a more extempore rendering of a shorter portion of the Word, more like our choruses of today.

There is nothing so glorifying to God as a singing saint, facing all of life's ups and downs with praise. We recall Paul and Silas singing at midnight in the prison in Philippi (Acts 16.25). When we sing we do not do so primarily to entertain one another but rather, as the verse makes clear, to praise the Lord. Not all have the same musical ability to sing well, but all should sing heartily and sincerely. Singing in worship should never be regarded as an incidental filler. It is a vital component of praise and thanksgiving offered to a kind and gracious God.

Heaven is full of the sound of singing.

5.20 - Praising

Giving thanks always for all things unto God and the Father in the name of our Lord Jesus Christ;

A thankful Christian finds reasons to thank God for everything, being constantly aware of His undeserved favour. Mentioning the Name of the Lord Jesus Christ is fitting because it is only through Him that sinners can be reconciled back to God and enjoy the rich bounty of every spiritual blessing in Him (Eph 1.3). As we count our many blessings from God, we are moved to give thanks. To be loved, forgiven, and on the way to heaven are blessings indeed; there are many more to come.

Temporal blessings should not be overlooked, including the provision of daily food, clothing, shelter, health, employment, family and friends. It is good always to pause before eating a meal and give God thanks for the food He has provided and for those who have kindly prepared it. This is one distinguishing mark of a life that honours God. It should be remembered that throughout the world millions of adults and children still go to sleep hungry, naked, and homeless.

The story of Job is intriguing. He was an upright and blameless man who was allowed to suffer greatly without knowing why. One day disaster struck swiftly and repeatedly in four heavy blows, leaving him bereft of his livelihood, his home, and all of his ten children. He responded in a remarkable way by falling down to the ground and worshipping God: "The Lord gave, and the Lord hath taken away; blessed be the name of the Lord" (Job 1.21). In his darkest hour, he was still thankful for all that God had previously given to him and he uttered not a word of complaint.

> *Begin the day with God;*
> *Kneel down to Him in prayer;*
> *Lift up thy heart to His abode,*
> *And seek His love to share.*
>
> *Converse in mind with God;*
> *Thy spirit heavenward raise:*
> *Acknowledge every good bestowed,*
> *And offer grateful praise.*

Be thankful first thing in the morning, be thankful last thing at night, and be thankful all through the day.

5.21 - Submission

Submitting yourselves one to another in the fear of God.

Spirit-filled Christians not only speak to one another about the goodness of God but they also submit to one another. God is a God of order and He expects that believers should respect and submit to the different levels of authority that are encountered in daily living, as described below. However, this particular verse goes beyond that and is not specifically concerned with levels of authority. It teaches that in all interpersonal relationships believers should exhibit a submissive spirit in their approachability and gentle reasonableness with one another. They are to assist and serve one another. Forceful dominance and an insistence in getting one's own way should be foreign to God's children.

In a wider sense, submission to godly order is necessary for the stability and blessing of society. Authority exists at different levels and in different spheres: the national ruler and his or her subjects; the employer and the employees; the husband and the wife; the parent and the child; the local church elder and the believer. God desires that we be law-abiding citizens, diligent employees, faithful spouses, obedient children, and cooperative believers in the local church. The devil aims to oppose and overthrow this order at every level. His interests are furthered by rebellion and anarchy, strikes, divorce, family breakdown, and strife and division in the Church.

Questions are always asked: what if the country's ruler is a tyrant, what if the boss unjustly exploits his workforce, what if a husband is an abusive drunkard, what if the parents are oppressive, and what if assembly elders are overbearing and harsh – must one submit to these injustices? The viewpoint of Scripture is clear: there is no licence to rise up and overthrow those in authority. However, there is room for stating one's case and then leaving the matter with the Lord (Acts 22.25). God has graciously given additional guidance in His Word for those who may find themselves in difficult situations (1 Cor 7.11).

Does this not turn Christians into spineless pacifists who condone sin and suffering? No! Christians are followers of Christ who endured unjust suffering and shame as no other ever has. They will refuse to do anything contrary to God's Word. In a day yet to come, God who is the righteous Judge of all the earth will do right (Gen 18.25). No injustice will go unpunished.

"In the fear of Christ" as it should be rendered, means to always be mindful of His glory and honour, and live to please Him. For His sake, we should treat one another with the utmost respect.

Meekness is not weakness; it is Christlikeness.

5.22 – As unto the Lord

**Wives, submit yourselves unto your own husbands,
as unto the Lord.**

The remaining verses of this chapter in Ephesians reveal God's plan and purpose for marriage. The general principle of Christian submission is applied specifically to the marriage bond. In a confused and contrary world, the truth about marriage as God intended it to be must be taught clearly and unapologetically.

Wives are to be subject to their own husbands. The phrase "submit yourselves", although absent from some early manuscripts, is here implied and follows on from the previous verse on submission. Paul is not building up an argument leading to a conclusion in this matter. He begins by stating the principle directly, having established the need for a submissive spirit in general among Christians, and then he will go on to explain the reasons for a wife's subjection.

Verses like this are often criticised as encouraging male chauvinism and the view that women are inferior. It is claimed that women are being deliberately suppressed and enslaved to men: in bowing and scraping before her spouse, the wife is losing her identity and dignity as an individual, is how the objection proceeds. Nothing could be further from the truth. In marriage and family life the woman acknowledges that her husband is to take the lead and she cooperates with God's plan. She accepts that this will bring blessing to all in her family including herself. Tampering with or amending the 'maker's instructions' is never a good idea. She submits to her husband because she knows that this is what is pleasing and honouring to the Lord.

Men and women, and indeed boys and girls, are equal in value to the Lord. There is no hierarchy in terms of worth. The essential distinction being addressed here is that they have different roles. Once this is understood, and each willingly and wholeheartedly takes up their respective roles, there is both harmony and stability.

In contradistinction to the views of the world at large, in which the exclusivity and permanence of the sacred covenant of marriage are scoffed at and belittled, the Bible emphasises the integrity of the marital bond by the term "your own husbands". The example of Aquila and Priscilla is outstanding – always together, always busy in God's work, and always encouraging God's people. Certainly, Paul and others benefitted from their kindness and hospitality (Acts 18.1-3, 26; Rom 16.3; 1 Cor 16.19).

A godly wife will always aim to please the Lord.

5.23 - Headship

For the husband is the head of the wife, even as Christ is the head of the church: and he is the saviour of the body.

The husband is head of the wife. This finds its origin in creation's order in that the man was created first, from the dust of the ground: "And the Lord God formed man of the dust of the ground, and breathed into his nostrils the breath of life; and man became a living soul" (Gen 2.7). It was the Lord God who saw that it was not good that the man was alone, therefore He determined to make him a suitable companion, "an help meet for him" (Gen 2.18). Using a rib from Adam's side, God fashioned Eve: "And the rib, which the Lord had taken from man, made he a woman, and brought her unto the man. And Adam said, This is now bone of my bones, and flesh of my flesh: she shall be called Woman, because she was taken out of Man" (Gen 2.22-23).

Paul also revealed a higher meaning in Christian marriage. It is to reflect the union between Christ and His Church. No other New Testament writer refers to this truth: Christ is Head of the Church which is His body (Eph 1.22; 4.15). He is to be honoured as such, as the members gladly do His bidding and follow His leading. They trust Him implicitly, knowing that He cares for them and will always direct them for their utmost good and blessing. They are assured of His constant love.

Christ as the Saviour of the body has a range of meanings. He loved the Church and proved it by redeeming it by His blood. He also continues to nourish and strengthen it through His present ministry at God's right hand. It is a matter of great wonder and comfort that the Saviour has not just saved us, but also promised to keep us and preserve us. He is there as our defender from the many dangers and enemies we might face. He is there in the moments of trial and sorrow. He is there to lift us up when we stumble and fall, and cheer us up when we grow discouraged. We are not left to wander home to heaven on our own. He is always with us and will never leave us nor forsake us (Heb 13.5).

Christ not only saves but He also keeps.

5.24 – Subjection to Christ

Therefore as the church is subject unto Christ, so let the wives be subject unto their own husbands in every thing.

Paul now explains how the Church's submission to Christ is an example of how wives should relate to their husbands. The Church willingly acknowledges its present dependence on Christ to provide for it and protect it. It knows already that He has proved His love in an undeniable way at the cross. The future challenges and difficulties that may lie ahead are also known to Him, and He can be trusted to lead and guide every step of the way.

The teaching concerning a wife's submission is open to all kinds of misunderstanding and there are those will strenuously oppose it, even in Christian circles. It must not be considered in isolation from all that Paul has to say on the subject of marriage, and specifically what he will go on to teach about the husband's role. For a wife to be subject to her husband in everything means that she will always give him his place as the head, and do so for Christ's sake. This does not include submitting or agreeing to anything that would be directly contrary to the Word of God.

In the normal course of family life, a wife may have her own opinion about a particular matter affecting the marriage and the family. Discussion is healthy and necessary between a husband and wife. Each may have a different perspective, and it is always a learning process when two individuals marry and begin to live together as one. A respectful exchange of ideas need not result in conflict; careful and patient listening will be necessary for both. Sometimes the wife has considered a side of things that her husband might have overlooked. A wise man will be humble enough to recognise this. But when all of the discussion is over, it is the husband who takes the lead as the head of the house. His wife should not mount a prolonged campaign of protest or resistance should her husband decide on a different course of action than the one she suggested.

There cannot be two heads in the household, just as there cannot be two monarchs on one throne, two chief executives of a single company, or two captains of a team. The conflict generated between two opposing forces can tear apart and destroy any institution, no matter how noble its aims might have been.

In marriage two become one, and the one is greater than the two.

5.25 – Love your Wives

Husbands, love your wives, even as Christ also loved the church, and gave himself for it;

The picture of marriage as God intended is now becoming clearer. If women consider that submitting to their husbands in everything is a difficult challenge, then what husband has not read these words about loving his wife in the way that Christ loved the Church and wondered if this might be nigh impossible.

Love is the adhesive that keeps marriages together and makes them work. It needs to be both expressed and demonstrated. The love in question is not some flighty infatuation or a dreamy state of bliss. This is practical, day-to-day love that is warm, vibrant and clearly seen. It is a wholehearted commitment to sacrificial giving for the good of another. The husband is to take the lead and set the tone for the marriage.

While we may fall short at times in our submission to Christ, there is no doubt that Christ's love for the Church was the greatest and highest expression of love that this world has ever seen. Giving has always been at the heart of divine love: "For God so loved the world, that he gave his only begotten Son" (Jn 3.16). Paul could speak of "the Son of God, who loved me, and gave himself for me" (Gal 2.20). God gave His best and Christ gave His all. Each one of us is so precious to Him that nothing was spared to make us His own: "He that spared not his own Son, but delivered him up for us all, how shall he not with him also freely give us all things?" (Rom 8.32).

Husbands are expected to sacrifice for their wives. This may involve a husband denying himself, especially if his wife has a particular need that requires financial resources. His thought of buying himself a new pair of shoes might have to be shelved for the time being. He may have to deny himself time to relax if she is busy preparing for guests to come and there is a lot of housework to be attended to. When she is ill, he will diligently serve her and attend to her special needs.

If a wife knows and sees that her husband is marked by unconditional love and care, she will have no difficulty whatsoever in submitting herself to him. Women gladly surrender to love.

Love gives, and gives, and gives.

5.26 - Cleansing

That he might sanctify and cleanse it with the washing of water by the word,

Christ is continuing the process of preparing the Church to spend eternity with Himself. The picture here extends beyond marriage, although purity and faithfulness are necessary for both. While a husband and wife can encourage each other in holiness, it is not the husband that sanctifies and cleanses his wife. By contrast, it is Christ who is cleansing the Church.

To sanctify the Church means that it is set apart for God and brought into conformity with His holy character. At conversion we became His exclusively. This is a positional truth that still requires a process to bring it to fulfilment. In the book of Revelation, the seven letters to individual local assemblies of believers in Asia revealed that there were commendable features but also certain characteristics that required correction. The eyes of Christ examined each one minutely and missed nothing. There were no perfect assemblies then, as now. The broader view of the Church shows a condition that is less than ideal; it is flawed and fractured so that, to our eyes at least, it does not yet appear as it should.

To cleanse the Church means to remove anything sinful or defiling. The new birth for each believer brought new life and the forgiveness of every sin. Each of us knows all too well that the tendency to sin remains, and we all make mistakes at times in what we think, say and do. The Holy Spirit of God through the Word of God brings to light these unholy things, and by God's grace, we as individuals and local churches corporately can progress and mature in holiness.

The washing of water by the word is the daily application of God's Word to our lives. (This does not refer to water baptism; baptism is a picture of death, burial and resurrection, but not cleansing.) This process of washing leads to a glorious outcome mentioned in the next verse. The Lord Jesus Christ indicated to His disciples in the upper room in Jerusalem that regular 'foot-washing' was necessary if continued fellowship with Himself was to be enjoyed. Later He prayed to the Father, "Sanctify them through thy truth: thy word is truth" (Jn 17.17).

Daily cleansing is necessary for the mind and heart,
not just for the skin.

5.27 - A Glorious Church

That he might present it to himself a glorious church,
not having spot, or wrinkle, or any such thing; but that it should
be holy and without blemish.

The ultimate purpose for Christ's Church is to be with Him for His pleasure and glory. This will be manifested at the marriage of the Lamb as described in Revelation: "Let us be glad and rejoice, and give honour to him: for the marriage of the Lamb is come, and his wife hath made herself ready. And to her was granted that she should be arrayed in fine linen, clean and white: for the fine linen is the righteousness of saints. And he saith unto me, Write, Blessed are they which are called unto the marriage supper of the Lamb" (Rev 19.7-9). This marriage is a future event that will take place in heaven after the Lord has come to the air for His Church and taken it home. Her fine linen attire will signify the righteous acts of the saints which they carried out for His glory while they were here upon earth. This is a reminder that one's testimony here upon earth has eternal significance.

Then again, when the Lord returns to the earth in power and glory to vanquish His enemies and set up His millennial kingdom, He will come with His Church. It will accompany Him in that day: "when the Lord Jesus shall be revealed from heaven with his mighty angels, in flaming fire taking vengeance on them that know not God, and that obey not the gospel of our Lord Jesus Christ ... When he shall come to be glorified in his saints, and to be admired in all them that believe" (2 Thess 1.7-10).

At present there are many spots and wrinkles in the Church – at least the part of it that can be seen upon earth. These terms indicate moral blemishes and imperfections. Each of us knows too that as individuals we are a work in progress; we have yet much to learn and further to go in the matter of holiness and conformity to Christ. Our Lord can see the end from the beginning and His purposes will be fulfilled.

What we weave down here, we will wear up there.

5.28 - Two as One

**So ought men to love their wives as their own bodies.
He that loveth his wife loveth himself.**

The word here to husbands is not based on the example of Christ but on a natural inclination and obligation to look after oneself. This love is not the narcissism of self-centred pampering but a healthy and necessary care for one's own body. This is an obligation that we all have, and those who are careless about the physical body God has given them are not a good testimony or example to others.

Paul is saying that the necessary care a man takes over his health and wellbeing is the same care he should devote to his wife. She should not be neglected in any way but given the best of his love and attention. When the apostle discusses marriage in 1 Corinthians 7, he explains his personal preference of singleness. He knew that most people marry and that his words concerning singleness were advisory rather than mandatory (1 Cor 7.6-7). But he does explain that an unmarried person is freer to focus on pleasing the Lord, whereas a married man must give time and effort in ensuring that he meets his wife's emotional and physical needs. This is not deemed as a fault but rather the husband's obligation in marriage: "But I would have you without carefulness. He that is unmarried careth for the things that belong to the Lord, how he may please the Lord: But he that is married careth for the things that are of the world, how he may please his wife" (1 Cor 7.32-33). In this context the "the things that are of the world" are not regarded as sinful; they are those necessary and legitimate things required to maintain a marriage. Finally, Paul is not suggesting that married people do not care at all for the Lord's things. He had married friends who meant a great deal to him and who were a sterling example of what Christianity should be in the home. They were certainly not second-rate in any way.

That a man loves himself when he loves his wife is another way of saying that the two have become one flesh. This is marriage as God intended from the beginning. Two lives are bound together as one, and each serves the other.

A husband should love his wife at least as much as he loves himself.

5.29 - Nourishing

For no man ever yet hated his own flesh; but nourisheth and cherisheth it, even as the Lord the church:

The parallels continue between a man's care of his own body and the Lord's care of the Church. Here Paul is stating the negative of what he has already stated positively concerning a man and his own physical body. If anything his language is even more forceful: 'not even one man ever thoroughly detested his own body'. Deeply rooted in each human personality is the motivation for self-preservation. Perhaps the only time when this may be absent is if the person is mentally deranged. Such a case would be the demon-possessed man from Gadara who lived among the mountains and tombs, and who was always crying out and cutting himself with stones (Mk 5.5).

Nourishing the body causes one to think of the constant care given to a dependent newborn infant, feeding it regularly and constantly tending to its every need. This process continues for many years, right through childhood. Beyond being a duty, it is characteristically administered in love. It produces bonding and mutual affection so that both emotional and physical needs are met.

The word for 'cherish' combines warmth, security, and tenderness. It is sometimes used of a hen brooding over her nest. In the Greek version of the Old Testament known as the Septuagint (LXX), the word is used in the translation of Deuteronomy 22.6, prohibiting a person from interfering should they come across a nest with a mother hen and her brood.

The only other time Paul uses the word is when he reminds the Thessalonian Christians of his burden of care for them. He truly parented his converts – it was not just a matter of seeing them profess faith and then promptly forgetting or abandoning them. He was like both a mother and a father to them; the first suggests his gentle care while the second denotes his firm counsel: "But we were gentle among you, even as a nurse [nursing mother] cherisheth her children"; "we exhorted and comforted and charged every one of you, as a father doth his children" (1 Thess 2.7, 11).

Our Lord is presently ministering on behalf of His people and caring for them. He is their Great High Priest, Shepherd, and Advocate. He understands their trials, He meets their daily needs, and He restores them when they stumble on the way.

The One who has lifted us up continues to bear us up on the journey home.

5.30 – His Body

**For we are members of his body,
of his flesh, and of his bones.**

This is a reassuring reminder of our position in Christ, as members of His body. He cares for it assiduously. The additional words, "of his flesh, and of his bones", if accepted as part of the original text, will be seen to be in line with Genesis 2.23 when Adam declared concerning Eve, "This is now bone of my bones, and flesh of my flesh".

In the Church, the body of Christ, every member shares in His life. Eternal life is the life of Christ within us. No one can adequately explain the fulness of this truth; every attempt seems inadequate. We are in Him and He is in us.

Christ nurtures and cares for us as individuals. He knows each of us intimately and so He can provide all that we need at any particular time. Each of us has a different and specific role to play as a member of His body, but He enables us to do whatever is required. This is amazing to comprehend when we consider the countless millions who have trusted in Him for salvation and committed their whole lives to Him. He has ministered to their every need.

We see this principle in action as Christ guided and strengthened His disciples, men of different backgrounds and abilities. They were at the same time a faithful remnant in Israel while being the first nucleus of the Church. We probably would not have chosen them, such a motley and unpromising group as they were. We certainly would never have had the patience that Christ afforded them as they stumbled along, misstepping here and misunderstanding there. In His hour of greatest need in Gethsemane, they fell asleep. After He was arrested, they ran away. Following His resurrection He found then cowering together because of fear (Jn 20.19), and yet, He went on caring for them as His friends (Jn 15.15).

We too are no better than the disciples and we must freely confess our many failings and shortcomings. Nevertheless, we are members of His body and He will never reject us nor forsake us. The challenge for us all is to get to know Christ better and to be more like Him in our daily living, so that we express the mind and will of Christ, our Head.

We are highly privileged to be members of Christ's body.

5.31 – One Flesh

For this cause shall a man leave his father and mother, and shall be joined unto his wife, and they two shall be one flesh.

The quotation is from Genesis 2.24 and states the basic principle of leaving and cleaving. The parental household is left behind and a new marital home is formed when a man is joined with his wife in marriage. The teaching of Genesis 2 is foundational for all marriages. Christian marriage is meant to have additional dimensions as has already been noted.

The leaving is important; this is a step in maturity. A man is no longer under the care of his parents and while he will always be responsible to respect and care for them if necessary, he has new priorities in caring for his wife and establishing a new household. In many cultures the parents may still seek to exercise control over their son or daughter; this can lead to conflict and strain within the new home.

To "cleave" conveys the idea of a firm commitment to be close and to remain together for life. They are 'glued' together! In marriage, a man needs a woman for him to be complete, and vice versa. They complement one another so that together they are a force for good. The Word of God gives no support to the attitude: 'I will give it a try; if it does not work out I can walk away.' God hates divorce and has said so: "For the Lord, the God of Israel, saith that he hateth putting away: for one covereth violence with his garment, saith the Lord of hosts: therefore take heed to your spirit, that ye deal not treacherously" (Mal 2:16).

"One flesh" includes the physical relationship, the emotional bond, and the volitional covenant before God. In Christian marriage, it also involves a spiritual unity so that when two people are united in their love for the Lord and share spiritual goals, they grow and serve together. If this element is not nurtured, spiritual stagnation can set in. Things can quickly unravel and fall apart when the Lord is not given first place.

Christian marriage is under attack from the devil. He realises the potential of a strong marriage and the blessing it can bring; he will do all he can to disrupt and destroy the harmony and unity of the home. We should pray often for newly married couples.

When marriage is truly in the Lord, it honours the Lord.

5.32 - A Mystery

This is a great mystery:
but I speak concerning Christ and the church.

Once again the word mystery appears in Ephesians. The Genesis account of the first marriage and the principles underlying it gave no hint of the deeper truth that would one day be revealed to the apostle Paul concerning Christ and His Church. And yet in retrospect, it is not difficult to see that Adam's deep sleep and the removal of his rib to fashion Eve foreshadowed the death of Christ and the price He paid for His bride, the Church. Eve owed her existence to Adam even as the Church owes hers to Christ. In relation to marriage, it has often been remarked that the bone was taken from Adam's side: not from his head that she might dominate him, and not from his foot that he might subjugate her. It was taken from his side so that the husband and wife should be together in loving support of one another.

The truth of the Church is not found in the Old Testament. While one can find pictures or illustrations of it in various Old Testament stories, there is no explicit teaching about it. The emphasis throughout is upon God's earthly people, Israel, from whom the Messiah would come. All changed with the coming of Christ. His national rejection as the King of the Jews resulted in His crucifixion. It also resulted in Israel being temporarily set aside in the plan of God.

In the furtherance of His kingdom programme, Christ instituted something completely new in the Church. The Church is made up of both Jews and Gentiles and its ultimate destiny is a heavenly one. From the day of Pentecost in Jerusalem (Acts 2) until that coming day of rapture when Christ returns to the air for His Church (1 Thess 4), He will continue to build the Church until it is complete. Today is a day of grace in which the gospel is being proclaimed to everyone everywhere.

To confuse Israel with the Church is to invite even more confusion. Many of the Old Testament promises made to the nation of Israel concerning the seed of Abraham, the promised land, the holy city of Jerusalem, and the throne of David await their fulfilment in the future millennial kingdom. The Church has not replaced Israel and cannot lay claim to these specific promises. It has so many wonderful promises of its own.

Christ and His Church are inseparable.

5.33 - His Wife, Her Husband

Nevertheless let every one of you in particular so love his wife even as himself; and the wife see that she reverence her husband.

This important section on marriage is brought to a conclusion with a summary of the main thrust of Paul's teaching – a husband's love and a wife's submission. The change of wording from "submit" to "reverence" is not as significant as it might seem. The two ideas are closely linked, conveying the idea of the wife respecting the husband's position as the one responsible to take the lead in the relationship.

A negotiated relationship, 'I will if you will', is bound to fail. It soon escalates to become, 'I won't because you won't', and this leads to an inevitable breakdown. That is why Paul does not tell husbands to make their wives submit to them; the husbands have one main responsibility and that is to love their wives unconditionally. The wives are not told to force their husbands to love them; their part is to submit to their husbands unconditionally. And as a general fundamental principle, both the husband and wife are to show love to one another and display a gentle submissive spirit.

Counselling before marriage is valuable and necessary. Local assembly elders, or perhaps the trusted Christian brother who will perform the wedding service, might be best qualified to do this. It is unwise to assume that the couple have already considered and understood the relevant Scriptures (Genesis 2; Ephesians 5; 1 Corinthians 7; and 1 Peter 3 would be the main ones). These can be read and simply explained. Other matters can be discussed, allowing time for questions and clarification if necessary. Practical matters can be raised such as communication in marriage, the management of finances, the intimate physical side of marriage, the rearing of children, and the couple's continued involvement in their local church and in the Lord's work.

Mature Christian couples should be on the lookout for the newlyweds, supporting them in prayer but also being particularly sensitive to any early signs that the marriage is in trouble. At times one is acutely aware of altered dynamics in a relationship. Prayerfully and carefully one might enquire, 'How are you getting on together? Would you care for a chat?' Much will depend on how free the husband or wife will be to respond to this opener. Preferably a young couple should be visited by another mature and caring couple. Great wisdom and discretion are required in all of these matters.

May our marriages glorify the Lord.

Chapter 6

Stand Firmer

Paul's final instructions concern family life and one's testimony in the workplace.
In view of the constant spiritual battle being waged, he encourages the believers
to stand firm and be fully armed against the foe.
His final greetings commend Tychicus, the bearer of the letter.

6.1 - Obedience

Children, obey your parents in the Lord: for this is right.

Family life is now considered, and certainly, Christianity must begin at home. If it does not work in the family setting, it has little chance of working anywhere else. Specifically, it is a Christian home that is being referred to here, "in the Lord", although the principle of obedience holds good for any family.

Children are addressed directly. The apostle is not saying, 'Parents, teach your children to obey you', but rather it is as if he expects that the children should be present when the letter is read out to the whole assembly. His instruction is brief but unambiguous; it is a call to obedience. This is one of the most difficult things for children (and adults) to do. All sorts of reasons and excuses are given for disobeying a straightforward instruction.

With man's fallen nature there is often an immediate and negative reaction to a clear command, causing a person to kick back at authority and do his or her own thing. This was exemplified in the Garden of Eden when Adam and Eve were told not to eat the fruit of the tree of the knowledge of good and evil. God warned of the outcome should they disobey, but graciously permitted them to eat the fruit of any other tree. We recall the sad result. Every parent has seen the same: the prohibition 'Don't touch' is often followed quickly by a transgression.

Obeying parents is not only right but also it is described in a parallel passage as being "well pleasing unto the Lord" (Col 3.20). Children are truly a blessing and heritage from the Lord (Ps 127.3), but they come with a heavy parental responsibility to train them in the ways of the Lord (Prov 22.6). This responsibility cannot be foisted upon anyone else such as a nanny or schoolteacher.

Family 'rules' should be simple, appropriate and fair. They also need to be consistently applied, with a follow-through if they are not heeded. A 'reward' for obedience is not inappropriate, especially with young children; it can positively reinforce good behaviour. But the parent who is always saying 'no' and majoring on negative commands may find that the child soon becomes deaf to this imbalance. Christian homes are to be places filled with love, warmth, security, and joy.

Childhood family memories stay with us throughout life.

6.2 - Honour

Honour thy father and mother;
(which is the first commandment with promise;)

This command is much wider than a call to obedience: it is an attitude of always giving parents their place and respecting them, even when they grow old and become frail and dependent. In the context of marriage, it was emphasised that the husband's clear priority is to love and care for his wife, but that does not absolve him from assisting his parents when they are in need. The same applies to a wife and her parents.

The readers are taken back to the giving of the Ten Commandments, one of which was "Honour thy father and thy mother: that thy days may be long upon the land which the Lord thy God giveth thee" (Ex 20.12; Deut 5.16). This fifth commandment is the only one with a specific promise of blessing attached to it.

The Scriptures are frank and direct about human weakness and family failings. Adam and Eve's son, Cain, was a murderer. Manoah's son, Samson, was self-indulgent and immoral. David's son, Absalom, was a rebel. Good men have had bad sons and paradoxically, some bad fathers have had good sons. Amon was an evil character whose son, Josiah, turned out to be a good king. This can be attributed only to the mercy of God. One reason cited for Israel's exile in Babylon was disrespect for parents (Ezek 22.7). God Himself complained before them, "A son honoureth his father ... if then I be a father, where is mine honour?" (Mal 1.6).

Perhaps every generation considers that standards are slipping and degenerating among the upcoming generation. Paul warned Timothy of moral decline when he wrote that "in the last days, perilous times shall come. For men shall be lovers of their own selves, covetous, boasters, proud, blasphemers, disobedient to parents, unthankful, unholy" (2 Tim 3.1-2). This was a sad pronouncement.

In the present day, family breakdown is common. What is more disturbing is that young children are being robbed of their innocence by those pushing their agenda. This has even included the suggestion that children can take their parents to court. An Indian businessman from Mumbai planned to sue his parents for giving birth to him without his consent, and consigning him to a life of suffering! Such is the moral perversity and insanity of our day.

Israel dishonoured God, their Father, and suffered the consequences.

6.3 - A Promise

**That it may be well with thee,
and that thou mayest live long on the earth.**

Paul adapted the original promise by omitting any reference to "the land". Originally, this was a specific promise to Israel regarding Canaan. The reference to a long life is a general principle, not an absolute one, regarding longevity. Some godly people have had short lives; this does not indicate that they dishonoured their parents. The Lord Jesus Christ could proclaim "I honour my Father" (Jn 8.49). His own life was cut short in its prime, only because He fulfilled His Father's will (Is 53.8; Jn 8.29).

Unquestioning obedience was how Christ responded to His Father. All of us must confess that this could not be said of ourselves. Our waywardness and selfishness at times must have grieved our parents. We learn and mature but slowly. Those who do seek to respect and care for parents can be confident that God, their heavenly Father, will be pleased by their faithfulness and will bless them. Families fall apart because they are being starved of such love and care. This includes 'Christian families' in which these basic principles of family life have been neglected. People are increasingly busy with seemingly urgent matters that cannot be deferred, but there is a tyranny in living a frantic life of crisis management. It can lead to more important and eternal issues bring overlooked.

Time is one of the most precious commodities. It has been said that parents of today would do well to give their children twice the time and half the money. Similarly, children should set aside time for their parents, even when they have left the family home and established their own household. There is really no excuse for losing touch.

Love grows when it is nurtured. A young child may think that his father is invincible, unbelievably strong and able to do anything. As years pass, the child matures and the father ages. One day the young man starts to realise that his father is no longer as strong or able as he used to be, but the son loves and respects him all the more. Mothers too appreciate in increasing measure their children's love and thoughtfulness in later life. Strong Christian families are a bright testimony in a darkening world. We should spare a thought for those who have never known the joy and comfort of having loving parents and a stable home.

Honouring parents is a lifetime responsibility.

6.4 - Raising a Family

**And, ye fathers, provoke not your children
to wrath: but bring them up in the nurture and admonition
of the Lord.**

In this verse the word 'fathers' can apply to both parents. They should be fair-minded and reasonable in their expectations and demands. Some try to relive their lives by proxy, expecting their children to achieve what they failed to do themselves when they were young. Children can rebel against such unreasonableness and grow up with deep-seated animosity against their parents. Even when filled with resentment, they keep striving to win the parental approval that never quite comes.

Another danger facing Christian families is hypocrisy. A father who is all politeness and pleasantness in the local assembly, but harsh and draconian as soon as he gets home, will scar his children. The same could be said of a mother who appears affable when out and about, but is always nagging her offspring at home. Such parents leave their children with the indelible impression that Christianity is all about keeping up public appearances, no matter what the true situation might be behind the facade.

Favouritism can be a problem as well; the Jacob-Esau scenario has been repeated many times over. Seeds of jealousy and deceit were sown by their parents in that divided home; the harvest reaped was suffering and strife for generations to come. All children are different, but they should know that they are loved equally and unconditionally, and appreciated for who they are as individuals.

We should both play and pray with them from early childhood. The 'family altar' seems threatened with extinction. The most convenient time and place used to be at the meal table, morning or evening, with the whole family present. The father would read the Bible and pray. The parents together with the children would briefly discuss what had been learnt from the Scriptures. A foundation of Christian values would be laid for the years to come, whatever the outcome might be. Safeguarding this precious heritage requires commitment and effort.

Children never forget their childhood experiences. These help to mould them. Good memories live on forever; bad memories persist as scars. The child who is shaped by the Word of God can, by God's grace, become the man or woman that will make a mark for God, in their home environment and even further afield.

Fill your child's mind with the Word of God.

6.5 - In the Workplace

Servants, be obedient to them that are your masters according to the flesh, with fear and trembling, in singleness of your heart, as unto Christ;

The good testimony of any believer in the workplace is of vital importance because others can be influenced to consider what makes this person different. They will be more open to listening to the gospel.

Paul was writing originally concerning the slave-master relationship and here he envisaged a Christian slave at work. The Roman Empire was built on the backs of millions of slaves. Roman citizens regarded manual work as being beneath their dignity so that often slaves outnumbered 'freemen'. One wealthy Roman had 20,000 slaves in his service, doing all the physical work and menial tasks on his estate. Slaves were bought and sold in the marketplace as a commodity and they were often regarded as less than human. The Roman writer, Varro, described them as one of three kinds of 'implements': vocal, or slaves; semi-vocal, such as oxen; dumb, such as wagons. Many masters were cruel and harsh and would punish their slaves severely for the most minor infraction. Those who pilfered could be branded on the face with 'CF' (*Cave furem* – Beware the thief). Stories exist of gruesome torture and death for nothing more than the sadistic pleasure of evil owners. However, other masters were kind and permitted their slaves to buy their freedom.

Laziness and carelessness were endemic among slaves; they were generally despised and often dispirited. However, Paul was pointing Christian slaves to a higher plane of service that commended their Lord. They were to be ever diligent in listening to and obeying their masters on earth. (The expression "according to the flesh" distinguishes physical, earthly masters from their one heavenly Master.)

The apostle was not encouraging Christian slaves to cower in a corner but "with fear and trembling" means serving their masters with due respect, being careful not to displease them. Such service was to be rendered sincerely and honestly. It was not to be done grudgingly or duplicitously, with feigned respect.

The last words, "as unto Christ", make all the difference. The service of the Christian slaves was to be carried out in the light of their faithfulness to Christ, honouring Him, their heavenly Master, while respecting their earthly masters. They were to be conscious that He observed all that they were doing. Every one of these principles holds good for Christian employees today.

Faithful Christian workers commend Christ in all that they do.

6.6 - Servants of Christ

Not with eyeservice, as menpleasers; but as the servants of Christ, doing the will of God from the heart;

God-fearing workers are conscious that the Lord is observing all that they do. One of the great tests of character is the integrity and quality of our lives when no other person is watching. This would apply also to the workplace, when the supervisor or boss is absent, or at least not directly observing what is going on and what one is doing.

The young slave Joseph maintained his integrity when his master was out of the house. The master's wife persisted in trying to tempt him to sin with her but Joseph refused and said, "Behold, my master wotteth [knoweth] not what is with me in the house, and he hath committed all that he hath to my hand ... how then can I do this great wickedness, and sin against God?" (Gen 39.8-9). For his loyalty and faithfulness, Joseph was rewarded with years of imprisonment after Potiphar's wife maliciously accused him of misconduct. He suffered unjustly for righteousness' sake, and yet God was in it all, moulding and maturing the young man to become eventually one of the greatest men who ever lived in the land of Egypt.

The apostle Peter, in addressing working slaves, pointed out that some masters could be unreasonable, and there was always the possibility of suffering unjustly: "Servants, be subject to your own masters with all fear; not only to the good and gentle, but also to the froward". He uplifted the example of Christ as one who suffered wrongfully at the hands of men (1 Pet 2.18-21).

The Christian is never really 'off duty'; Christ is always watching. This truth may at first seem burdensome, if one has a natural tendency to be a clock-watcher or slacker. On the other hand, there is a liberating quality in realising that everything I do – no matter what, no matter where, and no matter when – can be done for His glory. The artificial separation of life into the sacred and secular is completely done away with. We do not need to divide our week as is commonly done into Sunday for the Lord, Monday to Friday for my employer, and Saturday for myself. Our whole lives can be poured out for our Lord's pleasure and glory, and even the smallest thing done for Him becomes an act of worship.

Do all for Him, and do it wholeheartedly.

6.7 - Good Will

With good will doing service, as to the Lord, and not to men:

God is interested not only in what we do but also why we do it and how we do it. He sees into the heart and discerns our motives. Appearances do not deceive Him. This verse encouraged slaves to be ready and willing to attend to their duties. They should be wholehearted, as the previous verse suggests. Living in the fear of God makes a person conscious every day of God's presence and His all-seeing eye. The Christian slave was always to remember that above his earthly master there was a heavenly Master. He was serving both at the same time. 'Will it please the Lord?' was the most important question to be considered; the highest standard was to be maintained.

God is wholehearted in all that He does. In the prophecy of Jeremiah, the Lord reminded Israel of how He had appealed to them on many occasions to repent of their waywardness and sinfulness: "And now, because ye have done all these works, saith the Lord, and I spake unto you, rising up early and speaking, but ye heard not; and I called you, but ye answered not" (Jer 7.13). God in His mercy and grace promised to restore this undeserving nation: "I will give them one heart, and one way, that they may fear me for ever ... Yea, I will rejoice over them and do them good, and I will plant them in this land assuredly with my whole heart and with my whole soul" (Jer 32.39-41).

Christ too showed the same devotion and dedication to accomplish His work and fulfil the Father's will: "I have a baptism to be baptized with; and how am I straitened till it be accomplished!" (Lk 12.50); "My meat is to do the will of him that sent me, and to finish his work" (Jn 4.34). Thank God, He showed no reluctance to accomplish our salvation.

Christian employees should be diligent and faithful in giving of their best. In a parallel passage in Colossians, Paul put it this way: "And whatsoever ye do, do it heartily, as to the Lord, and not unto men" (Col 3.23). May we follow the example of our Lord in whatever work we must do and avoid being like the nobles of the Tekoites in Nehemiah's time who "put not their necks to the work of their Lord" (Neh 3.5).

Half-heartedness is an insult to the Lord.

6.8 - The Reward

Knowing that whatsoever good thing any man doeth, the same shall he receive of the Lord, whether he be bond or free.

Significantly, neither Paul nor any other New Testament writer was a vocal campaigner against slavery in the way that activists might encourage today. However, Christian principles applied equally to masters and slaves, or employers and employees as we might say. These principles upheld the essential dignity and value of each individual while recognising their different roles. An acknowledgment was made that some masters might be unreasonable and harsh, and other slaves might be lazy and dishonest, but God's children, whether masters or slaves, were expected to act differently.

The letter that Paul wrote to his friend, Philemon, concerning the runaway slave Onesimus, is full of interest. There is no reason to suspect Philemon of having been a cruel master. However, Onesimus had probably stolen from him before running away to Rome, a cosmopolitan city thronging with all kinds of people from all over the empire. He could be virtually anonymous there, finding freedom and at the same time escaping justice. He would have known that slaves could face the death penalty for such crimes as he had committed. But Onesimus had not reckoned with the grace of God, for in Rome he heard the gospel and was converted.

Paul wrote to Philemon, a tender plea, asking him to receive back the erring slave. He offered to recompense Philemon for any loss he had incurred. He also reminded Philemon that Onesimus was now "a brother beloved ... in the Lord" (Philem v. 16). The master and his slave would remain in their respective roles, but they were now bound together as one by the love of Christ. These few words were alien to the general mindset and institution of slavery as commonly practised in Roman times.

There was something else for the Christian slave to keep in mind: the Lord would give to every one of His servants an appropriate reward. This anticipates the future Judgment Seat of Christ when the Lord will take into account the way His children have upheld their testimony and honoured Him, even in the workplace. By this measure, we must anticipate that heaven will be full of surprises. Those who seemed quiet and insignificant workers in the office or on the factory floor, diligently getting on with the job in hand, might well be revealed as people who brought the most pleasure to His heart.

Faithful labour will not be overlooked in heaven.

6.9 - The Master in Heaven

And, ye masters, do the same things unto them, forbearing threatening: knowing that your Master also is in heaven; neither is there respect of persons with him.

In a brief but pointed manner Paul also addressed the other side of the equation: how the Christian master should behave in his dealings with his slaves. The common practice, as has been discussed, was to mistreat slaves and regard them as less than human. Slavery and the gross mistreatment of employees still exist in all societies, with vulnerable people being exploited and abused.

Societies have at times been influenced by the philosophies of men in total disregard for God and His Word. Old-style communism denied the need for God and claimed that all men were equal: class distinctions, including those in the workplace, could be done away with. So much for the high-minded theory; the practice was far different and produced a privileged ruling class more tyrannical than anything that had gone before under the tsars. Modern variants of such philosophies are no better. The pride and greed of the human heart have not been dispelled by the vaunted wisdom of men.

Christian masters were here enjoined to be just as conscientious and diligent as their slaves in fulfilling their role. They were expected to be fair and reasonable. Verbal abuse particularly was to be repudiated – shouting, insulting, mocking, and threatening. It is telling to observe how employers speak to their most junior staff, how the CEO greets the doorman as he enters his headquarters, and even how we talk to others who may be employed by us at any time. This verse indicates that God shows no respect of persons in His dealings with men.

Many slaves did not receive a wage. Their provision of living quarters, food and clothing was expected to be sufficient. Those who did earn a wage might eventually purchase their freedom. While the matter of wages is not dealt with here, the apostle James condemned the rich men who used hired labour and cheated their workers when it came to payment (Jas 5.4). God heard the cries of those who were exploited in this way.

The Christian master would have to give an account before the Lord, his own Master, of how he treated those in his service. A high and equal standard was required of both employer and employee.

Both master and slave must give a full account to the Lord.

6.10 - A Call to Arms

Finally, my brethren, be strong in the Lord, and in the power of his might.

In addition to the teaching about marriage, family life, and the Christian's testimony at work – requiring believers to be controlled by the Holy Spirit and submissive to one another – Paul had a further vital matter that had to be addressed. It concerned all believers, not just husbands and wives, parents and children, masters and slaves. Every believer has a daily spiritual battle with a wily enemy, the devil. We ignore this truth at our peril. The Christian life is not like an afternoon picnic, a 'fun run', or a pleasure cruise – it is an uphill and lifetime struggle against a formidable foe who would cast us down if he could, and leave us languishing in the dust of defeat. We are in a fierce, unrelenting conflict against the devil.

The previous chapters have brought to light God's purposes to bless in Christ, to unify in the Church, to enable through the Spirit, and to sanctify through the truth. In view of this, we now consider His provision to strengthen for the battle. A new believer, seeking to be faithful in living an obedient, God-honouring and Christ-exalting life, will soon face opposition from within and from without. He still has the flesh within; the world and the devil surround and press upon him from without. These three mortal enemies are constantly on the attack.

Being strong in the Lord is a command to avail oneself of the spiritual power that is available from Him. Paul had already written of the nature of that divine power as demonstrated in the resurrection of Christ (Eph 1.19-20). Again he had prayed that they might be "strengthened with might by his Spirit in the inner man" ((Eph 3.16). The power of the Christian is not his own; it is "in the Lord", the power of the Holy Spirit who enables him. In terms of the spiritual battle that must be fought, that power is made available when we follow the Holy Spirit's guidance and do His will according to the Word of God. He will cause our efforts to be effective.

God's mighty power ("the power of his might") will always confound the enemy. God is omnipotent; the devil is not. For our part, we need to be humble, conscious of our weakness and inability, and be obedient to our Commander who has already defeated the foe at Calvary. We dare not waver or try to be neutral.

We are to be willing volunteers in God's army,
not reluctant conscripts.

6.11 - Stand Firm

Put on the whole armour of God, that ye may be able to stand against the wiles of the devil.

To be able to stand against the enemy requires that the believer be fully equipped and protected by a complete set, or panoply, of armour. The success of world empires such as the Greek or Roman empires was in large measure a result of their military might and the superior equipment of their soldiers.

The Christian soldier must be fully armed. This is an urgent command from the captain of our salvation, the Lord Himself (Heb 2.10). The soldier cannot afford to leave any vital organ unguarded because the devil is a master strategist who seeks out and exploits any vulnerability that he can find. His tactics are varied so that he may try a direct assault, but if this fails, he has more subtle means at his disposal. He attacks God's people from without and also from within, using external persecution or internal disagreements. He knows too that moral failure will advance his cause by weakening the Church from within. He is always trying to divide and rule.

In the early days of the Church, these alternating tactics were much in evidence. External challenges came from the authorities who tried to prohibit the believers from spreading the gospel. The religious rulers in Jerusalem said to one another, "Let us straitly threaten them, that they speak henceforth to no man in this name", but Peter boldly replied, "we cannot but speak the things which we have seen and heard" (Acts 4.17, 20). Internal challenges came from moral weakness such as the deceit of Ananias and Sapphira (Acts 5), or the friction between different cultures, as when there were complaints of partiality in the distribution of aid to widows (Acts 6).

On a personal level, the devil is constantly trying to trip us up. Those who are lazy and prefer to leave the fighting to others, he can leave well alone; they pose no threat to his schemes. But for those on active service, He knows the personal weaknesses, their Achilles' heel, which he exploits to the full. To neutralise them he also uses diversionary tactics: if they can be distracted to focus more on earthly pursuits – furthering their education, advancing their career, accumulating wealth, or indulging in pleasure, sport or entertainment – rather than pursuing spiritual goals, then he gains the advantage. Paul said of the enemy that "we are not ignorant of his devices" (2 Cor 2.11).

Remember, you do not stand alone on the battlefront.

6.12 - The Battle Arena

For we wrestle not against flesh and blood, but against principalities, against powers, against the rulers of the darkness of this world, against spiritual wickedness in high places.

As to the nature of the Christian's conflict, it is not principally a physical one upon earth but rather a persistent spiritual struggle against powers that inhabit the realm above, the "high places" in the heavenlies. Leaving the image of modern warfare aside in which bullets, artillery and missiles are fired from a distance, this verse is describing the believer's personal battle against spiritual enemies as unrelenting hand-to-hand combat at close quarters. It is a daily fight that knows no end upon the earth, for there is "no discharge" in this war (Eccl 8.8).

Paul does not identify four different enemies but rather the totality of the forces arrayed against the believer. These would be the devil and his fallen angels in the realms above, but also include men and women of earth who are under the devil's control and who advance his cause. Down through the centuries, there have been infamous tyrants who have railed against God and His people, putting many believers to death. While these might be regarded in one sense as "flesh and blood" opposition, the point is that they all took their orders from another realm. The real power behind them was satanic.

Paul recalled in another letter that he "fought with the beasts at Ephesus" (1 Cor 15.32). There are well-attested records of Christians being thrown to the lions and other wild animals for the sadistic entertainment of others, but it is more likely that Paul had in mind those people who were vigorously opposed to his ministry (Acts 19).

Satan is not omnipresent but his influence is everywhere. Angels who rebelled with the devil are now his emissaries throughout the world. These spiritual enemies are living on borrowed time in that they have already been defeated by Christ at Calvary: "having spoiled principalities and powers, he made a shew of them openly, triumphing over them in it" (Col 2.15). Satan and his foes must have thought that when the Saviour died they had been victorious. The empty tomb and the risen Christ soon dispelled that premature conclusion.

The repetition of the word "against" shows the need to be strong and maintain our stand. Darkness and wickedness abound. Only in Christ are we assured of victory.

While we remain on this earth, we are in the battle.

6.13 - Fully Equipped

**Wherefore take unto you the whole armour
of God, that ye may be able to withstand in the evil day,
and having done all, to stand.**

Since the fall of Adam and Eve into sin, there has never been a day that was not evil; the trajectory of the human race has been inexorably downwards. Philosophers and scientists may argue that such progress has been made in human development and understanding so that religion has been made obsolete. Christianity is only a crutch for the emotionally weak and intellectually challenged; faith is nothing more than a fanciful exercise in self-delusion, so they say.

The clear evidence is that sin and evil abound and even in the most 'enlightened' progressive nations, those who are responsible to maintain law and order are hard-pressed to cope. Often the politicians and leaders who claim to represent the interests of the people are themselves exposed as men and women who are driven by self-interest and a lust for power and wealth. Their high ideals are only for 'the other man'.

The believer has no choice but to live in society and yet engage in the spiritual battle. Spiritual warfare is not an option; it is a necessity. This urgent command is to arm oneself fully with what God has provided and boldly take a stand for the Lord. While all around us there is evil, at times one faces a particular crisis when the enemy comes in "like a flood" (Is 59.19).

A thrilling story emerged from the Israeli-Arab Yom Kippur War of 1973. Israel was caught unawares and the nation was in peril as hundreds of Syrian tanks advanced on the Golan Heights. In the heat of the crisis, a lieutenant called Zvika Greengold rushed to the battlefront in a damaged Israeli tank. Because of enemy action he had to change tanks several times. He fought for over twenty hours, often single-handed, and destroyed tens of enemy tanks before retiring exhausted, covered with burns, wounds and soot. He would later recount that 'I was not scared of dying. I was scared of failing.' He also recalled a moment in the heat of battle when he realised that he was surrounded by the enemy and felt completely alone.

The battle the Christian must wage is unrelenting and even more critically, it has eternal consequences. However, Christ's soldiers will never be alone and their armour will never fail. The apostle Paul wrote of a particular time in his experience when all men forsook him, nevertheless, he attested that "the Lord stood with me, and strengthened me" (2 Tim 4.17).

Christ was alone in His darkest hour; He will never abandon us in ours.

6.14 - The Belt and Breastplate

Stand therefore, having your loins girt about with truth, and having on the breastplate of righteousness;

The armour is spiritual, not physical, and here two key defensive components are identified. The repeated call to stand implies urgency and preparedness; it is more 'take a stand' than just remain standing. The prevailing darkness, wickedness and evil demand it.

Girding the loins was not simply an act of decorative adornment. The belt was an essential item for combat and helped to secure the whole suit of armour. It had side-hooks for attaching other equipment and it was fronted by a short leather apron. It was also used to hitch up the tunic or robes so as not to impede free movement in the battle. Of course what Paul is referring to here is mental preparation: grasping the truth that God has revealed in His Word and allowing the truth to take a grip of us. It can hold us steady so that we remain faithful and true to Him. Peter referred to girding up "the loins of your mind" (1 Pet 1.13).

Before Joshua entered the promised land to begin his military campaign, God encouraged him in the truth of His Word: "The book of the law shall not depart out of thy mouth; but thou shalt meditate therein day and night, that thou mayest observe to do according to all that is written therein: for then thou shalt make thy way prosperous, and then thou shalt have good success. Have not I commanded thee? Be strong and of good courage ... for the Lord thy God is with thee whithersoever thou goest" (Josh 1.8-9).

The breastplate protected vital organs, the heart and lungs, from a frontal attack. It has often been remarked that there was no special protection mentioned for the back, suggesting that the Christian soldier is urged to face forwards at all times and never to turn round and retreat. If he does so he will be vulnerable. Other historical records indicate that the breastplate, especially if made of chainmail, could have had a back portion as well.

There is no need to choose between the positional righteousness that the believer has in Christ from the moment of conversion, and the practical conditional righteousness that he acquires in following the example of Christ. Both belong together: having the first requires us to appropriate the second by seeking always to do what is right in God's sight.

Truth and righteousness are our first line of defence.

6.15 - The Footwear

**And your feet shod with the preparation
of the gospel of peace;**

In the First World War, the effectiveness of many of the infantry soldiers was related to the condition of their feet. Weeks of immersion in mud and water left many crippled with 'trench foot', a painful and debilitating infection. Their mobility was compromised and this meant that they were a liability rather than an asset. An estimated 75,000 British soldiers died from this condition in that terrible conflict.

We must now consider the sense in which the Christian soldier's 'feet' are protected by spreading the gospel of peace in a time of war. The first point is that those who are focused on making known the gospel are preserved from indolence. They do not have time to squander because they are busy seeking the welfare of lost souls, whereas the devil finds work for idle hands to do.

Gospel-minded believers also avoid an unhealthy and negative preoccupation with others, particularly discussing the faults and failings of their fellows. When Peter asked the Lord about John, "Lord, and what shall this man do?", the Saviour corrected him by saying "If I will that he tarry till I come, what is that to thee? follow thou me" (Jn 21.21-22). We might paraphrase it as 'Mind your own business, Peter. Just make sure that you are following me'.

Those who proclaim the gospel far and near are advancing into enemy territory. They know that a soul converted to Christ is a captive set free from Satan's dominion. The gospel itself is the power of God unto salvation and the devil will do all he can to silence the bold preachers of the cross. In the time of the early Church it was so, and it has remained so until this day.

While there is much bad news in circulation, the gospel has always been a message of good news – life and liberty, forgiveness and reconciliation, peace and security, hope and assurance. The gospel herald, motivated by love for Christ and love for souls, is sure-footed in the battle. He has a clear goal and direction, always forwards and upwards. He will not slip and slide and lose his way. God describes such feet as being beautiful: "How beautiful upon the mountains are the feet of him that bringeth good tidings, that publisheth peace; that bringeth good tidings of good, that publisheth salvation" (Is 52.7).

Always be ready to tell of Christ.

6.16 - The Shield

Above all, taking the shield of faith, wherewith ye shall be able to quench all the fiery darts of the wicked.

One additional piece of equipment was vital. The Roman soldier was protected by a large full-body shield. Paul links this to the principle of faith. The exercise of faith is instrumental in a person becoming a Christian: "For by grace are ye saved through faith" (Eph 2.8); subsequently, it is also active along life's pathway: "For we walk by faith, not by sight" (2 Cor 5.7). At the end of life upon this earth, it is that which gives hope and assurance of a glorious future. It is faith at the beginning, faith at the end, and faith right the way through.

By faith, great exploits have been accomplished by God's children in the past. They were fully aware of their personal weakness and inability, but through faith they were made strong and bold in the knowledge that the mighty Lord was with them. 'Faith sees the invisible, believes the incredible, and receives the impossible.' Faith allows us to see what others cannot see. In the time of Elisha, the prophet, a great array of Syrians forces encompassed the city of Dothan. Elisha's servant was in panic mode, fearful of the outcome. Elisha prayed "Lord, I pray thee, open his eyes, that he may see." The Lord answered the prophet's prayer and the young man perceived a mighty army on their side, just as Elisha had said: "Fear not: for they that be with us are more than they that be with them" (2 Kings 6.16-17).

One of the tactics used in ancient warfare was to dip arrowheads in tar or some other ignitable material and set these alight, before firing them in the direction of the enemy. If they hit their target, they would inflict terrible injury, both piercing and burning their victims. The devil, the wicked one, is a ruthless and brutal opponent; he has many fiery darts at his disposal. These can be launched suddenly, catching the unsuspecting combatant off-guard. The only sure defence is the shield of faith. It is reassuring to note that Paul is affirming that not one enemy dart will reach its target when this shield is employed.

One of the most effective military formations was when Roman soldiers were trained to stand close together on the front line, holding their shields before them, with the ranks behind holding their shields above their heads. While they maintained this united front, they were safe; should any of them break ranks they became vulnerable.

There is strength and safety in believers standing shoulder to shoulder.

6.17 - The Helmet and Sword

**And take the helmet of salvation,
and the sword of the Spirit, which is the word of God:**

The helmet protects the head and metaphorically, the mind, so that here salvation itself is considered as one of our defences in the battle. Salvation has past, present, and future aspects. All of these aspects can be enjoyed daily; they strengthen us for the fight. In retrospect, we can look back to the 'moment' of salvation, that time when we believed in Christ and were completely forgiven. We were saved from the penalty of our sins so that we could never be lost. What encouragement comes from this assurance! The present aspect of salvation can be realised every day in that the believer can know deliverance from the power of sin. Then, in prospect, the Christian knows that one day he will be delivered from the presence of sin, when the battle has been fought and he is safely home in heaven. A mind fortified by all of these truths will be protected from discouragement and doubt. In another scripture, Paul emphasised the sure hope of salvation as a protective helmet (1 Thess 5.8).

The sword mentioned here was the short dagger that was sharp on both sides; it could be used for stabbing or slashing movements at close range. Two divine resources available to every believer are the indwelling Spirit of God and the inspired Word of God, the Bible. The Spirit uses what we know of God's Word, bringing to our minds verses and truths that are appropriate for every occasion. The example of the Lord Jesus Christ can never be equalled: during His temptation in the wilderness, when He was alone and physically weak from fasting, He countered three attacks from the devil by quoting from the book of Deuteronomy. Each time He answered with authority and began by saying, "It is written ..." (Mt 4.4-10).

Unless we learn to read the Word daily and apply it to our own lives, we will always be weak and vulnerable. It is our daily food to strengthen us for the day ahead. It is our daily light to guide us through the darkness. It is our armour to protect us in the fray. The sword was used not only for defence but, as stated above, it was also a weapon for offence. The early apostles took the fight to the enemy with boldness and clarity. Like the Lord, they applied the Old Testament scriptures to their hearers with devastating effect.

May we learn to use the sword of God's Word effectively.

6.18 – Constant Prayer

Praying always with all prayer and supplication in the Spirit, and watching thereunto with all perseverance and supplication for all saints;

There is little point in a soldier being well armed if he is not well deployed, as to place and time, on the battlefield. In all armies there must be clear lines of communication and command. Generally speaking, the Commander-in-Chief has ultimate authority in terms of strategy and goals, but under him are many levels and officer ranks through which the commands are passed. When there is a breakdown in this chain of command, disaster and defeat are not far away. For this reason, modern warfare will often focus on disrupting enemy communications.

At the bottom of the rankings, the lowly foot soldier will rarely have any direct contact with the Supreme Commander, whereas, in the battle that every Christian must fight, each has the privilege of direct contact with the Lord. While he must be respectful of others (parents, employers, and spiritual shepherds too), no other rank needs to be involved. His orders are received directly; his own requests are heard immediately. In both instances, the soldier of Christ is dealt with in love and grace.

Through prayer, we can be in touch with the Lord every moment of the day. That we should have definite times of daily prayer is vital, but that we should freely and constantly breathe the atmosphere of prayer throughout the day is just as important. (Notice the four 'alls' in the verse). Paul encourages us on all occasions to keep in touch with God, bringing our urgent requests before Him whenever necessary. The specific word the apostle uses here is only applicable to believers coming before God and speaking to Him; it does not apply to seeking human advice. The first is our priority; the second is optional and may not always be appropriate. It is the Holy Spirit within us who enables, energises, and directs our prayers.

We need to be always alert to the need of the hour, and also vigilant as to the schemes of the enemy. We dare not fall asleep at our post. Loving concern for the needs of others similarly engaged in the battle, will make us prayer warriors in support of our fellow soldiers. We should eagerly and persistently seek their best interests, particularly when they have particular problems to deal with such as illness, bereavement, disappointments and trials. We stand or fall together.

Remember to pray for fellow soldiers.

6.19 - A Personal Request

**And for me, that utterance may be given unto me,
that I may open my mouth boldly, to make known the mystery
of the gospel,**

The letter to the Ephesians is saturated with praise and prayer. There are the two major prayers of the apostle which soar upwards and heavenwards, seeking fulness of spiritual blessing for the believers. We have just considered Paul's exhortation to be vigilant in prayer, just as the Lord Jesus had commanded His slumbering disciples before He faced the battle alone: "Watch and pray, that ye enter not into temptation: the spirit indeed is willing, but the flesh is weak" (Mt 26.41).

Paul made a personal request for prayer support in the work of the gospel. It is all the more poignant, having being written from prison. His location had not changed his vocation; he was still intent on proclaiming the gospel and he knew that this demanding ministry required clarity and boldness. He could not rely upon past success; each new venture required fresh supplies of divine grace and power.

The apostle never maintained an aloofness from others; he was one with them in all the stresses and strains of working for God. He never implied that only they were the weak ones who needed prayer and fellowship, and that he could do without such things because he was strong enough on his own. Mutual support was vital.

When Paul wrote to the Christians at Rome, he had in a similar way opened his heart and mind to them, and had beseeched them to pray earnestly for him: "Now I beseech you, brethren, for the Lord Jesus Christ's sake, and for the love of the Spirit, that ye strive together with me in your prayer to God for me" (Rom 15.30). His first specific request was for preservation from his many enemies because of the physical dangers he faced. His second was for his acceptance by the saints in Jerusalem, some of whom may have doubted his sincerity. Finally, he had a deep desire to visit them and become personally acquainted with them.

The mystery of the gospel here is perhaps a more general term than that which has gone before in the letter. It includes all that the gospel reveals to sinners of their need, all that Christ has done to meet that need, and all that the gospel will accomplish for the glory of God.

> *Yes, we are always wondering, wondering how*
> *Because we do not see*
> *Someone, unknown perhaps, and far away*
> *On bended knee.*
>
> F. M. N.

6.20 - An Ambassador

For which I am an ambassador in bonds: that therein I may speak boldly, as I ought to speak.

There have been several references already to Paul's imprisonment: he was a prisoner for their sakes, and also a prisoner for the Lord's sake (Eph 3.1; 4.1). Here he is a prisoner for the gospel's sake, and at the same time, he has the honour of being an ambassador for Christ (cf. 2 Cor 5.20). An ambassador is one who has been commissioned to represent his sovereign in a foreign land. He is to be loyal and faithful. In many ways he is like his sovereign, embodying and portraying all that is good and true about his home country: the language, dress, beliefs and customs. He always stays in touch with the homeland and at the end of his term of duty, he must return and give an account of his service.

Paul's imprisonment in Rome was in the form of house arrest. It lasted two years and the house was one he hired himself (he had to pay the rent) while all the time being guarded by a Roman soldier. Usually, the guards changed duty every four hours. They were themselves in effect a 'captive' audience, probably hearing much of what Paul had to say. Apart from being held in custody, Paul had considerable liberty to receive and converse with friends and guests

(Acts 28.30-31). What is clear is that he witnessed to all who came into contact with him, "Preaching the kingdom of God and teaching those things which concern the Lord Jesus Christ, with all confidence, no man forbidding him." Some were saved as a result of his unique opportunities (Acts 28.23-24; Phil 1.13; 4.22). It is likely too that the runaway slave, Onesimus, encountered Paul the prisoner in Rome and was converted there.

He prayed, not for his release from prison but for continued freedom, clarity and boldness in proclaiming the gospel. It was a matter of necessity as well as urgency for Paul. On another occasion he wrote, "woe is unto me, if I preach not the gospel!" (1 Cor 9.16). When it came to the harsh final imprisonment before his execution, Paul's passion and fire had not dimmed as he wrote to Timothy, "Preach the word; be instant in season, and out of season" (2 Tim 4.2).

We all are ambassadors for Christ.

6.21 - Tychicus

**But that ye also may know my affairs, and how I do, Tychicus, a
beloved brother and faithful minister in the Lord,
shall make known to you all things:**

In a spirit of fellowship and reciprocal care, Paul informed the Ephesian Christians that his colleague, Tychicus, would update them on his situation. While we should be reticent to major on 'I, me, and mine', there are those who like to know all the details about the affairs of others, but who are secretive and economical about disclosing anything of themselves, and not always for reasons of humility. Paul was being transparent while remaining truly humble. He prayed for the Ephesians and hoped that they would intercede for him in his heartfelt need. He was deeply interested in their spiritual welfare and he anticipated that they would equally be interested in his state and condition. True fellowship requires balance and openness.

Tychicus was the courier of both the letter to the Ephesians and also the letter to the Colossians in which he is described as a fellow servant (Col 4.7). It is possible that he also recorded this letter for Paul. Often the apostle used a scribe or secretary to write down his thoughts as he narrated them (Rom 16.22). There is some evidence that Paul suffered from an eye disease which made it difficult for him to write, but in any case, it was customary for him to personally append his signature (1 Cor 16.21; Gal 6.11; 2 Thess 3.17; Philem v. 19).

The commendation of Tychicus was affectionate and fulsome as a "beloved brother and faithful minister in the Lord". He was a trustworthy friend and companion. Three times over Paul indicates that Tychichus would relay the news to them. He had accompanied Paul to Judaea in AD 57, when the apostle had gone to Jerusalem to deliver a gift to help the believers during a time of famine. He is identified as a native of Asia and might himself have been an Ephesian like Trophimus (Acts 20.4; 21.29).

Paul had so many friends who assisted him and whom he gladly commended. We all owe so much to others who have loved us and prayed for us, supported us and encouraged us every step of the way. Eternity will reveal the difference they made.

Tychicus was a true friend to Paul, being both loved and loyal.

6.22 - Comfort

Whom I have sent unto you for the same purpose, that ye might know our affairs, and that he might comfort your hearts.

There is a great need for the ministry of comfort and encouragement. In this case, it would be ministered to the Ephesians by Tychicus after completing his long journey to them. When he had rested and refreshed himself, he would have sat down alongside the Christians and related to them all the news concerning Paul in prison. Earlier in the epistle, the apostle had expressed his anxiety that they should not faint and become discouraged because of his circumstances (Eph 3.13). Paul's friend, Epaphroditus, was also one who was distressed to think of the reaction of the Christians at Philippi after they had heard he had been seriously ill. Here is the essence of Christian love, a concern for the thoughts and feelings of others.

Paul had so many disappointments and discouragements, and yet without bitterness, he could simply relate that he was sometimes alone and forsaken, and at other times he suffered greatly because of the evil opposition of his enemies (2 Tim 4.10, 14, 16-17). What grace to recount such events in an attitude of meekness and acceptance! His only comfort was in the Lord who stood by Him.

God is described as "the Father of mercies, and the God of all comfort" (2 Cor 1.3). In tribulation and affliction He is ever near. One of His purposes in allowing His children to pass through deep waters is that they might be able to comfort others.

The Lord Jesus Christ, God's only Son, is our "merciful and faithful high priest" who was made like us, sin apart, and He is able to succour and assist us in all of our trials. He understands and is touched with the feeling of our infirmities so that when we flee to Him in prayer, we find mercy and grace to help in our time of need (Heb 2.14, 17-18; 4.14-16).

Finally, the Holy Spirit was described by Christ as "the Comforter" (Jn 14.16, 26; 15.26; 16.7). Christ promised that after He left His disciples to return to heaven, He would send the Holy Spirit. The idea behind the word 'comforter' is of one called to our side to assist us in a time of need. There is not only comfort in a time of trial but also encouragement to keep moving forwards.

Mutual encouragement is a necessity.

6.23 - Peace

**Peace be to the brethren, and love with faith,
from God the Father and the Lord Jesus Christ.**

Christians are not belligerent but they are engaged in a battle that is not of their choosing; it is one that must be fought for the Lord's sake. They are followers of the One who came as the Prince of Peace and whose message is the gospel of peace. Faith in Christ brings us into a relationship of peace with God, and subsequently peace and unity with other believers. Paul had already urged the believers to strive to maintain that unity in the bond of peace. His final greetings convey the force of his deep desire and hope for them: not only peace, but also love with faith. These three Christian blessings form a strong triad. God the Father and the Lord Jesus Christ are linked together in the equality of deity as the source of these blessings.

Strife and division occur among believers when the flesh holds sway. The devil quickly detects any unprotected area should a foot soldier of Christ fail to arm himself with the full suit of protective garments and weapons. Any chink will be exploited at the earliest opportunity. The enemy knows our individual weaknesses and also the vulnerabilities of any company of Christians. Certainly, doctrinal disagreements have troubled the unity of the Church since the first century, but other weaknesses can threaten unity. Moral laxity, worldliness, pride and love of prominence were already present when John addressed the seven churches in Asia in the book of Revelation.

Significantly, a departure from their "first love" was the main criticism brought to the attention of the church at Ephesus in the book that John wrote a generation later (Rev 2.4). In many other ways they had maintained their orthodoxy in doctrine and diligence in service, but they were suffering from a serious heart condition that required emergency treatment. They were called upon to repent without delay, otherwise, they would be quickly judged and their lampstand of testimony removed.

So much of Christian service can be carried out mechanically, without love. Busyness can be associated with barrenness. Like the fig tree that Christ condemned, there can be foliage without fruit (Mt 21.19). In our lives we need to be honest in our self-assessment and allow the Spirit of God to search our motives. Rekindling our love for Christ Himself will yield eternal fruit in our own lives and bring blessing to others.

Love is at the heart of Christianity.

6.24 – Grace

**Grace be with all them that love our
Lord Jesus Christ in sincerity. Amen.**

In the inspired writings of the apostle Paul, one cannot escape the truth of grace in all its forms. His characteristic opening and closing greetings are pervaded by a sense of man's unworthiness being met with God's undeserved blessedness.

God has been gracious in that He has revealed Himself to all mankind. There will be none who can claim that He left them in complete darkness. The whole tenor of the first chapter of the Epistle to the Romans is to show that all men receive some light, and God will hold them accountable according to their response. In creation, and through conscience, God has spoken even to those who have never heard the gospel. The Gentiles are "without excuse" is the conclusion (Rom 1.20). The Jews had special privileges but they too fell short of God's holy standard.

"All have sinned" has been answered by the "all" of matchless provision in the death of Christ: "He that spared not his own Son, but delivered him up for us all, how shall he not with him also freely give us all things?" (Rom 8.32). God's righteousness is received through faith in Christ "unto all and upon all them that believe: for there is no difference" (Rom 3.22). Where sin did abound, grace has much more abounded.

Unlike God's grace and love to us, which have no variation or limitation, our love can often waver and fall short. Therefore, the final greetings express a hope that the believers' love might not be corrupted but be constant and unfailing. These parting words assume an added poignancy in light of the subsequent history of the church at Ephesus. God's love has been poured into us so that it will flow out of us, to our fellow-believers, our families and friends, and to a lost world that needs to hear that God loves them too.

The word 'Amen' is often used in conclusion; it means 'let it be so'. It denotes emphatic agreement with the truth that has been declared and anticipates that it will come to pass. And so it is, having begun our ascent of the letter to the Ephesians, we have climbed higher towards the majestic peaks of revealed truth. We freely admit that we cannot fully comprehend the scale and beauty of all that we have seen, but we can rejoice that in the wonderful purposes of God we have been included.

Grace reigns!

Review

God's Purposes Revealed

Drawing the many threads of truth together, we can summarise the main purposes of God as revealed in the letter to the Ephesians. Several of Paul's prayer requests have been included; under the inspiration of the Holy Spirit, all of them perfectly reflect the divine will.

God's purposes for Himself:
to receive praise and glory eternally (Eph 1.6, 12, 14)

God's purposes for Christ:
to be the Head of the Church (Eph 4.15; 5.23)
to be the universal Head of all things (Eph 1.10, 22)

God's purposes for the Church:
to unite Jew and Gentile in one body (Eph 2.16; 3.6)
to reveal the manifold wisdom of God (Eph 3.10)
to be a holy dwelling place for God (Eph 2.21-22)
to be submissive to Christ (Eph 5.24)
to be sanctified and presentable (Eph 5.26-27).

God's purposes for the Christian:
to be holy and blameless (Eph 1.4; 4.22-24)
to walk worthily (Eph 4.1)
to be knowledgeable about divine blessings (Eph 1.18-19; 3.19)
to live sacrificially (Eph 5.2)
to be kind and forgiving (Eph 4.32)
to be loving husbands (Eph 5.25)
to be submissive wives (Eph 5.22)

to be considerate parents (Eph 6.4)
to be obedient children (Eph 6.1)
to be fair employers (Eph 6.9)
to be faithful employees (Eph 6.5)
to be loyal soldiers (Eph 6.10)

God's purposes for all of Creation:
to be consummated in Christ (Eph 1.10)

Reflection

The Ascent of Everest by John Hunt is a classic piece of adventure writing, and for me, it was an exciting boyhood read. It relates the first successful expedition to reach the top of the world's highest mountain. This was achieved on 29th May, 1953, when two men, Edmund Hillary and Norgay Tenzing, traversed the final ridge to the summit at 11.30 a.m. They spent about 15 minutes there, taking photographs and enjoying the panoramic view of the vast Himalayan range below. After burying some sweets and a small cross in the snow, they began their descent. The news of their triumph was wired back urgently to Britain and released on the morning of the coronation of Queen Elizabeth II. Hunt's book relates the months of careful planning, the many personnel involved, the united teamwork, and the numerous businesses and companies that provided supplies, logistical support and financial assistance. It was truly a combined effort on a colossal scale. Somewhat enigmatically, Hunt ended his book with this line: 'There is no height, no depth, that the spirit of man, guided by a higher Spirit, cannot attain.' These words sound familiar!

While in no way denigrating the courage and skill of those who achieved such distinction, the fact remains that all their efforts culminated in only two individuals enjoying the view from the top of the world, and that for a very short time indeed. By contrast, we who have spent time and effort 'ascending' Ephesians can rejoice at the great purposes of God for all those who have trusted in Christ as Saviour. We have wondered at God's planning from before creation; we have marvelled at the price that Christ paid for us in blood; and we have been comforted to know of our support from the entire Godhead – Father, Son, and Holy Spirit – elevating each of us to sonship, uniting all of us in one body, and blessing us abundantly with the immeasurable riches of Christ. Indeed, we all have shared the majestic view from 'the heavenlies'. While we enjoy these truths now, the coronation day is coming when the whole world will acknowledge the greatest achievement ever known, that which God has accomplished in Christ. This will be *the news* that will resound for all eternity.

I'm pressing on the upward way,
New heights I'm gaining every day;
Still praying as I'm onward bound,
"Lord, plant my feet on higher ground."

I want to scale the utmost height
And catch a gleam of glory bright;
But still I'll pray till rest I've found,
"Lord, lead me on to higher ground."

Lord, lift me up, and let me stand
By faith on Canaan's tableland;
A higher plane than I have found,
Lord, plant my feet on higher ground.
Johnson Oatman Jr.

Life's Greatest Quest
by Clark Logan

ISBN 9781904064954

Available from:
www.ritchiechristianmedia.co.uk

Christianity in Action
by Clark Logan

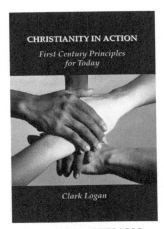

ISBN 9781907731990

Available from:
www.ritchiechristianmedia.co.uk

His Voice in the Morning
by Clark Logan

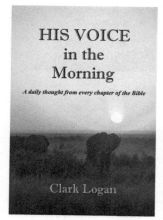

ISBN 9781910513873

Available from:
www.ritchiechristianmedia.co.uk

Cover to Cover
by Clark Logan

ISBN 9781912522392

Available from:
www.ritchiechristianmedia.co.uk